THE COTSWOLDS'
FINEST GARDENS

THE COTSWOLDS' FINEST GARDENS

TONY RUSSELL

To Jean.
very best wishes.
Tony Russell.
June 2012.

AMBERLEY

Sezincote – The Water Garden

First published 2009

Amberley Publishing Plc
Cirencester Road, Chalford,
Stroud, Gloucestershire, GL6 8PE

www.amberley-books.com
Principal photographer Tony Russell; text and
photographic copyright © Tony Russell, 2009

The right of Tony Russell to be identified as the
Author of this work has been asserted in accordance
with the Copyrights, Designs and Patents Act 1988.

ISBN 978 1 84868 702 8

British Library Cataloguing in Publication Data.
A catalogue record for this book is available from the
British Library.

Typeset in 10 pt on 12 pt TheAntiqua.
Typeset by FonthillMedia™.
Printed in the UK.

Photo Page 1 – Sudeley Castle Gardens
Photo Page 2 – City of Bath Botanical Gardens

INTRODUCTION

Although we regularly bemoan the climate of the British Isles, it has undeniably helped us create a country rich in gardens. As editor of the annual publication *Gardens to Visit* and through my broadcasting, writing and consultancy work, I am regularly visiting gardens across the length and breadth of Britain and find myself continually in awe of the wonderful diversity of garden styles – spanning more than one thousand years of gardening – that Britain has to offer.

Nowhere, in my opinion, is this diversity more evident than in the Cotswolds, a region long recognised as being the home of some of Britain's greatest gardens. It is, therefore, quite surprising that, until now, few publications have managed to clearly demonstrate the astonishing horticultural diversity that exists here.

Living and working in the Cotswolds for the past twenty years has allowed me ample opportunity to get to know not just the famous gardens, but all the gardens which abound in this quintessential part of England. Here, amidst gently rolling hills, steep, wooded valleys and fast-running streams, there are gardens of every kind imaginable, representing virtually every style of garden design and every period of garden history from medieval monastic gardens to twenty-first-century cosmic gardens. Where else can you find American, Chinese, Japanese, Persian-Indian, Amazonian and, of course, English-style gardens, all within a stone's throw of each other? The difficulty for me has not been in searching out gardens to include in this book, but more in deciding which gardens to leave out. Fifty may sound an abundance of gardens, but in truth, I could have included one hundred and fifty.

I make no apologies for the final selection; they are for me the finest of their genre and tell the tale well. You, the reader and garden visitor, will judge if that is the case.

All the gardens within this book allow public access, at least for some period during each year. So, please enjoy this book and the stories it tells and then go out and enjoy the wonderful gardens that the Cotswolds has to offer.

Tony Russell
Autumn 2009

❁ THE LIST OF GARDENS

❀ THE LIST OF GARDENS

FEATURED GARDENS

ABBEY HOUSE GARDENS
Market Cross, Malmesbury,
Wiltshire SN16 9AS
Tel: 01666 827650
www.abbeyhousegardens.co.uk

ABBOTSWOOD
Stow-on-the-Wold,
Gloucestershire GL54 1EN
Tel: 01451 830173

ALDERLEY GRANGE
Alderley,
Gloucestershire GL12 7QT
Tel: 01453 842161

ALGARS MANOR
Iron Acton,
South Gloucestershire BS37 9TB
Tel: 01454 228372

**AMERICAN MUSEUM IN
BRITAIN**
Claverton Manor,
Bath, Somerset BA2 7BD
Tel: 01225 460503
www.americanmuseum.org

BARNSLEY HOUSE
Barnsley, Cirencester,
Gloucestershire GL7 5EE
Tel: 01285 740000
www.barnsleyhouse.com

**CITY OF BATH BOTANICAL
GARDENS**
Royal Victoria Park, Upper
Bristol Road, Bath,
Somerset BA1 2NQ
Tel: 01225 396386
www.bathnes.gov.uk

BATSFORD ARBORETUM
Batsford Park,
Moreton-in-Marsh,
Gloucestershire GL56 9AB
Tel: 01386 701441
www.batsarb.co.uk

BERKELEY CASTLE GARDENS
Berkeley, Gloucestershire GL13 9BQ
Tel: 01453 810332
www.berkeley-castle.com

BLENHEIM PALACE
Woodstock,
Oxfordshire OX20 1PP
Tel: 01993 811091
www.blenheimpalace.com

BOURTON HOUSE GARDEN
Bourton-on-the-Hill,
Moreton in Marsh,
Gloucestershire GL56 9AE
Tel: 01386 700121
www.bourtonhouse.com

BUSCOT PARK
Faringdon,
Oxfordshire SN7 8BU
Tel: 01367 240786
www.buscotpark.com

CERNEY HOUSE GARDENS
North Cerney, Cirencester,
Gloucestershire GL7 7BX
Tel: 01285 831300
www.cerneygardens.com

COLESBOURNE PARK
Colesbourne, Near Cheltenham,
Gloucestershire GL53 9NP
Tel: 01242 870264/567
www.snowdrop.org.uk

COTSWOLD WILDLIFE PARK
Burford
Oxfordshire OX18 4JW
Tel: 01993 823006
www.cotswoldwildlifepark.co.uk

DAYLESFORD HOUSE
Daylesford, Moreton-in-Marsh,
Gloucestershire GL56 0YH
Tel: 01608 659888
www.daylesfordorganic.com

DYRHAM PARK
Dyrham, Nr Chippenham,
Wiltshire SN14 8ER
Tel: 0117 937 2501
www.nationaltrust.org.uk

EASTLEACH HOUSE GARDENS
Eastleach Martin, Cirencester,
Gloucestershire, GL7 3NW

**ERNEST WILSON
MEMORIAL GARDEN**
Leasbourne, High Street,
Chipping Campden,
Gloucestershire
www.ChippingCampden.co.uk

HIDCOTE MANOR GARDEN
Hidcote Bartrim,
Chipping Campden,
Gloucestershire GL56 6LR
Tel: 01386 438333
www.nationaltrust.org.uk

HUNTS COURT
North Nibley, Dursley,
Gloucestershire GL11 6DZ
Tel: 01453 547440

**IFORD MANOR – THE PETO
GARDEN**
Bradford on Avon,
Wiltshire BA15 2BA
Tel: 01225 863146
www.ifordmanor.co.uk

KELMSCOTT MANOR
Kelmscott, Lechlade,
Gloucestershire GL7 3HJ
Tel: 01367 252486
www.kelmscottmanor.org.uk

KEMPSFORD MANOR
Near Fairford,
Gloucestershire GL7 4EQ
Tel: 01285 810131
www.kempsfordmanor.co.uk

KIFTSGATE COURT GARDEN
Chipping Campden,
Gloucestershire GL55 6LN
Tel: 01386 438777
www.kiftsgate.co.uk

THE MATARA GARDENS
Kingscote Park,
Kingscote,
Gloucestershire GL8 8YA
Tel: 01453 860084
www.matara.co.uk

FEATURED GARDENS

MILL DENE GARDEN
Blockley, Moreton inMarsh,
Gloucestershire GL56 9HU
Tel: 01386 700457
www.milldenegarden.co.uk

MISARDEN PARK
Miserden, Stroud,
Gloucestershire GL6 7JA
Tel: 01285 821303
www.misardenpark.co.uk

NEWARK PARK
Ozleworth, Wotton-under-Edge,
Gloucestershire GL12 7PZ
Tel: 01453 842644
www.nationaltrust.org.uk

OWLPEN MANOR
Uley, Dursley,
Gloucestershire GL11 5BZ
Tel: 01453 860261
www.owlpen.com

OZLEWORTH PARK
Ozleworth, Wotton-under-Edge,
Gloucestershire GL12 7QA
Tel: 01453 845591

**PAINSWICK ROCOCO
GARDEN**
Painswick,
Gloucestershire GL6 6TH
Tel: 01452 813204
www.rococogarden.org.uk

**PRIOR PARK
LANDSCAPE GARDEN**
Ralph Allen Drive, Bath,
Somerset BA2 5AH
Tel: 01225 833977
www.nationaltrust.org.uk/
priorpark

RODMARTON MANOR
Cirencester,
Gloucestershire GL7 6PF
Tel: 01285 841253
www.rodmarton-manor.co.uk

ROUSHAM
Near Steeple Aston, Bicester,
Oxfordshire OX25 4QX
Tel: 01869 347110
www.rousham.org

RUSKIN MILL
Old Bristol Road, Nailsworth,
Gloucestershire GL6 0LA
Tel: 01453 837500
www.rmet.co.uk

SEZINCOTE
Near Moreton in Marsh,
Gloucestershire GL56 9AW
Tel: 01386 700444
www.sezincote.co.uk

SNOWSHILL MANOR
Near Broadway,
Gloucestershire WR12 7JU
Tel: 01386 852410
www.nationaltrust.org.uk

STANCOMBE PARK
Stancombe, Dursley,
Gloucestershire GL11 6AU
Tel: 01453 542815

STANWAY HOUSE
Winchcombe, Near Cheltenham,
Gloucestershire GL54 5PQ
Tel: 01386 584469
www.stanwayfountain.co.uk

STONE HOUSE GARDEN
Wyck Rissington, Near
Cheltenham,
Gloucestershire GL54 2PN
Tel: 01451 810337
www.stonehousegarden.co.uk

**SUDELEY CASTLE
GARDENS**
Winchcombe, Near Cheltenham,
Gloucestershire GL54 5JD
Tel: 01242 602308
www.sudeleycastle.co.uk

THE OLD RECTORY
Duntisbourne Rouse,
Daglingworth,
Cirencester
Gloucestershire GL7 7AP

THROUGHAM COURT
Througham, Near Bisley,
Gloucestershire GL6 7HG
Email:cafacer@netcom.co.uk
www.christinefacer.com

TORTWORTH COURT
Tortworth Court Four Pillars
Hotel, Near Wotton-under-Edge,
Gloucestershire GL12 8HH
Tel: 01454 263000
www.tortworth-court-hotel.co.uk

TRULL HOUSE GARDEN
Near Tetbury,
Gloucestershire, GL8 8SQ
Tel: 01285 841255
www.trullhouse.co.uk

UPTON HOUSE
Banbury, Oxfordshire OX15 6HT
Tel: 01295 670266
www.nationaltrust.org.uk

UPTON WOLD
Northwick Estate,
Near Moreton in Marsh,
Gloucestershire GL56 9TR
Tel: 01386 700667

**WESTONBIRT
THE NATIONAL ARBORETUM**
Westonbirt, Near Tetbury,
Gloucestershire GL7 2RW
Tel: 01666 881200
www.forestry.gov.uk/westonbirt

**WESTONBIRT
SCHOOL GARDEN**
Westonbirt, Near Tetbury,
Gloucestershire GL8 8QG
Tel: 01666 881338
www.westonbirt.gloucs.sch.uk

THE MAP OF GARDENS

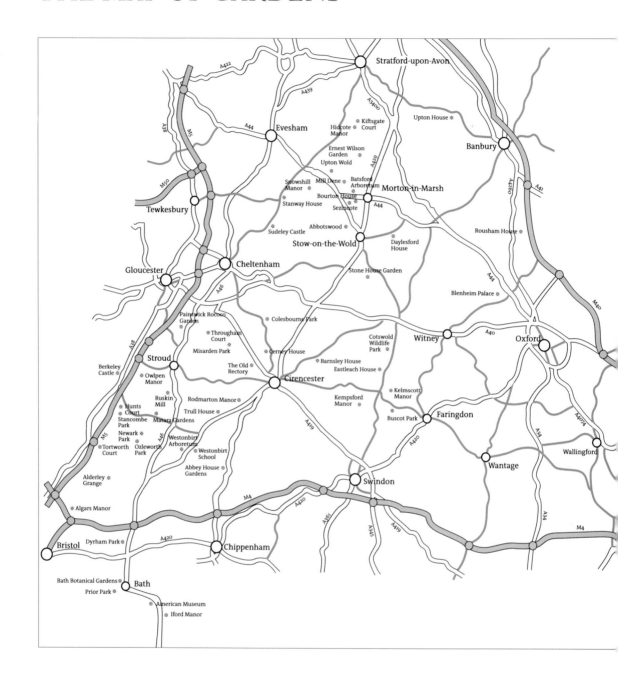

✿ ABBEY HOUSE GARDENS

With over one thousand years of history, the burial place of an English King, knot gardens, herb gardens, a river walk, monastic fishponds, a waterfall inspired by the leaping carp pool in the grounds of Kinkaku-ji (the Golden Temple in Kyoto, Japan), over 2,000 different roses (believed to be one of the largest collections in the UK) and 100,000 tulips, this spectacular 5-acre garden is without doubt one of the Cotswolds' finest horticultural achievements.

It is a glorious mix of ancient and modern and lies at the very centre of Malmesbury, one of the oldest boroughs in England having been given royal borough status around AD 880. Overlooking the gardens are the remains of the twelfth-century abbey, which once had a spire taller than that of Salisbury Cathedral. The present day Abbey House Gardens are the creation of Barbara and Ian Pollard (otherwise known as 'The Naked Gardeners' because of their penchant for gardening 'au naturale'), who purchased the property in 1994 and began gardening in earnest in the autumn of 1996. ▸

The gardens at Abbey House

❁ ABBEY HOUSE GARDENS

◀ Visitors to the garden today will be astonished at just what has been achieved in such a short period of time. Close-clipped yew hedging has been used to replicate the original walls of the abbey (which at one time extended across one third of the garden) and now provides both living divisions for a series of diverse garden rooms and an evergreen foil for rainbow-esque floriferous borders and carefully placed, thought-provoking sculpture. The knot garden is a triumph, taking a Celtic cross design from St Martin's cross on Iona in the Western Isles and using traditional plantings of cotton lavender, box and wall germander, alongside purple berberis, to create an intricate pattern of great beauty.

Away from the house and its relatively formal garden layout, the land plunges down a series of terraces bedecked with heathers, auriculas, camellias, rhododendrons and acers to the bank of the River Avon where marginal bog plants and Tasmanian tree ferns follow its sinuous meanderings. From here a bridge leads across the Avon to a modern-day 'tumpe' complete with a circle of staddle stones surrounded by Dutch and bearded iris. Close by, a waterfall with leaping carp stone – a Japanese symbol for perseverance – adds a further dimension to this remarkable garden.

◀ The Saxon arch   The Celtic Cross Knot Garden

13

✿ ABBOTSWOOD

In 1900, Mark Fenwick, a Gloucestershire banker with a passion for plants and gardening, purchased Abbotswood House and engaged Edwin Lutyens to design a garden 'appropriate to the house'. On Lutyens' arrival, his first glimpse of the house led him to suggest to Fenwick that he should, 'blow it up and start again'! On reflection, Lutyens felt the house was not beyond redemption, but required a major face-lift if it was to lend itself to the garden he wished to create. This face-lift included the introduction of an imposing two-storey gable with eaves that swept dramatically down to shoulder-height. Once complete, Lutyens turned his attention to the garden, producing a design that allowed for a seamless transition from the house to the garden with architectural features in both reflecting the other.

More than 100 years later, the gardens at Abbotswood are considered one of Lutyens' greatest achievements and a Mecca for disciples of his work. There is a fine loggia attached to the house that leads directly to a paved stone terrace, below which a Cotswold-stone-pillared pergola runs alongside a box-edged parterre and rose garden. Elsewhere, there are sunken gardens, colour gardens, pools, fountains and a typical Lutyens three-sided outdoor 'room' – a Cotswold-stone summerhouse – with a roofline to reflect that of the main house. Beyond the formality, Lutyens 'borrowed' the sloping land to the south-west and created a series of vistas from the formal garden to the rolling hills beyond. ▶

Lutyens' box-edged rose garden

Abbotswood water garden ▶

❈ ABBOTSWOOD

◂ Perhaps his finest feature is the lily pool garden located directly beneath a pediment window in the western gable of the house. It is Lutyens through and through and shows how a house and garden can become entwined within the same design.

Beyond the Lutyens garden, Abbotswood has a further 20 acres of glorious gardens, largely created by Mark Fenwick, including a heather garden; a stream garden of pools, cascades and rapids; a woodland ravine planted with bamboos, Japanese maples and azaleas; and a small arboretum.

The Blue Garden

✿ ALDERLEY GRANGE

Located in the peaceful Cotswold village of Alderley on the south-west edge of the Cotswold escarpment, this privately owned Grade II Historic Garden, surrounding a fine seventeenth-century property, is full of charm and elegance in a completely unpretentious way. In summer, the garden is an absolute joy, awash with fragrance and colour, especially when the roses are blooming in June and early July. The present garden structure was established by the late Alvilde Lees-Milne, a renowned plantswoman and designer who owned and lived in the grange until 1974.

It is suggested that she was aided in this work by Vita Sackville-West and there are several plants in the garden which originate from Sissinghurst. On either side of the eighteenth-century garden wall, Alvilde created pleached lime walks, herbaceous borders, hexagonal herb garden and planted roses in profusion, mainly old-fashioned varieties including many climbers; some of which scramble across a delightful seventeenth-century wooden gazebo, which rests contentedly in a corner of the walled garden. ▸

Across the rose garden to the pleached lime walk

✤ ALDERLEY GRANGE

◀ In 1974, the present owners, Mr and Mrs Guy Acloque, came to the property and continued to build on Alvide's work, showing deference to the original concept but bringing something of themselves to the original structure. Guy, a keen and knowledgeable gardener, has rejuvenated the original herbaceous borders, created a new herb garden and filled the lower garden, close to the greenhouse, with aromatic foliage plants including Californian allspice *Calycanthus occidentalis* and camphor. Although very much in favour of a relaxed feel to the garden and indeed gardening in general – 'gardening should be like a German gentleman's haircut, you are never aware that it has happened' – Guy has added his own formal statement to the garden with a series of clipped privet orbs, which help provide boundaries for the surrounding informality.

Alderley is a garden that must not be rushed, its delightful air of tranquillity positively insists that time is taken to absorb every vista, scent and flower. In the centre of the lawn is a characterful old mulberry tree, believed to have been planted in 1608 and contemporary with the house. It certainly looks its age and a graceful recline has been arrested from a complete collapse by a series of metal braces and clamps.

◀ The rose garden

Seventeenth-century wooden gazebo

✾ ALGARS MANOR

Despite being situated close to the south-western edge of the Cotswolds, Algars Manor cannot truly be described as a typical Cotswold garden. Here the soil and plants combine to create something more Cornish than Cotswold. In a secluded valley complete with stream, pockets of free-draining sandy soil ensure ericaceous favourites such as rhododendrons, camellias, azaleas and magnolias thrive, and in spring there are relatively few Cotswold gardens that come even close to rivalling its beauty.

Although Algars Manor has been in existence since 1610, the garden today is the creation of Dr John Naish, a former Second World War naval doctor who moved to the area in 1950. Finding an ornamental garden of high maintenance, he quickly decided it was not the garden for a busy doctor with little time to spare and set about turning it into a woodland garden of flowering trees and shrubs, something akin to Caerhays Castle in Cornwall, where magnolias reign supreme. ▸

Magnolia time at Algars Manor

Cherry blossom in profusion ▸

◀ Today you can wander beneath arching branches dripping with deep claret-purple cups of *Magnolia liliiflora* 'Nigra'; *Magnolia* 'Pinkie' with purple-red cup-shaped flowers which fade to a rich pink after a few days; *Magnolia* 'Ricki' which can only be described as a glorious 'Ribena' colour and *Magnolia* 'Susan' with its delightful slender, cerise-coloured, tulip-like blooms. In all there are scores of magnolias to enjoy, along with Japanese flowering cherries, rhododendrons and camellias, all planted on a south-facing bank, which descends to a fast-running tributary of the River Frome.

Throughout this garden, which covers approximately two acres, there are many choice, rare and quite simply stunning spring flowering plants to enjoy, including tender, yellow-flowered Australasian mimosas *Acacia dealbata*, vibrant red-barked trees such as *Arbutus menziesii* from Vancouver Island and a stunning South American Chilean Firebush *Embothrium coccineum*. Algars Manor is truly a beautiful garden and one that demonstrates the horticultural skill and love for plants of its creator John Naish.

After a long and fruitful life, John passed away during the summer of 2009; his garden lives on as a fitting memorial to a remarkable man.

The late Doctor John Naish with his wife Barbara

✾ AMERICAN MUSEUM IN BRITAIN

Located just to the east of Bath, on the southern-most edge of the oolitic limestone stratum which makes up the Cotswolds, is one of the region's best kept garden secrets. Here, high on the escarpment, in an area of outstanding natural beauty with spectacular views across the valley of the River Avon, is Claverton Manor, the home of the American Museum.

The museum, which first opened to the public in 1961, houses the only collection of American decorative arts outside the United States. Surrounding the manor are 120 acres of grounds containing formal and informal gardens, an arboretum, orchard and ancient meadows studded with veteran oaks and cedars.

Quite naturally, much of the planting throughout the grounds is of North American origin, but given the plant diversity to be found in this continent there is nothing wrong with that, far from it, as it helps provide a fascinating historical insight into many of the plants we now commonly grow within British gardens. ▸

The replica of George Washington's garden at Mount Vernon

◀ At the very centre of the garden is a unique replica of George Washington's famous garden at Mount Vernon in Virginia. A gift from the delightfully named 'Colonial Dames of America' in 1962, the garden is enclosed by a white picket fence and made up of a series of ornamental flower-beds, bordered by close-clipped box hedging. Pear trees and old-fashioned roses bring height to the garden, and in one corner (as in the original garden) is a reproduction of the octagonal wooden schoolhouse used by Washington's step-grandchildren.

Close by is a colonial herb and vegetable garden, containing dye plants and vegetables known to have been grown by both George Washington and Thomas Jefferson. Beans, squash, pumpkins and gourds formed much of the staple diet for the early settlers.

The eight-acre arboretum contains a fine collection of American trees and shrubs including many East Coast maples, West Coast conifers and several specimens of *Magnolia grandiflora*. A particularly fascinating addition to the garden is the Lewis and Clark Trail, which includes a selection of the flora discovered by the two American explorers during their expedition of 1803 to 1806, which attempted to find a natural navigable water route across America from the Atlantic to the Pacific.

◀ The Colonial schoolhouse

The American Museum in Britain

❊ BARNSLEY HOUSE

If there is one view from one Cotswold garden which is recognised the world over, then it is probably the view of the laburnum walk with wisteria, underplanted with alliums, at Barnsley House, the former home and garden of the late, and much missed, garden designer and author Rosemary Verey. The combination of that long, yellow tunnel rising from drifts of hazy pink-purple is just sensational, and during her lifetime was undoubtedly one of her 'signature tunes'.

The 4-acre garden which Rosemary created from 1961, around the seventeenth-century Cotswold family home of her husband and architectural historian, David Verey, was one of the most influential gardens of the late twentieth century. Her ability to mix garden styles and periods in a seamless and delightfully aesthetic way was admired unreservedly by her peers, as was the way she was able to make relatively small areas feel much larger through the clever use of perspective, plants and architecture. Island and peninsular borders, full of layers of carefully chosen colours and textures, were used both to create vistas and subdivide the garden into individual areas, each with its own distinctive character. ▶

Carefully chosen colours and textures

The Laburnum Walk in May ▶

❉ BARNSLEY HOUSE

◀ Almost as well known as the laburnum walk, Rosemary's potager, or kitchen garden, made up of numerous box-bordered beds containing an ornamental blend of vegetables and aesthetic plantings, influenced a whole generation of gardeners.

Rosemary Verey died in 2001 and for a while the future of her garden looked uncertain. However, in recent years Barnsley House has changed ownership and the house transformed into a country-house hotel and restaurant.

The current owners are very aware of the importance of the garden and its horticultural legacy and have retained members of the original gardening staff to ensure its continuation. Of course, over time plants will die and need to be replaced and no garden should remain frozen in time – Rosemary herself would fully subscribe to that – but it is hoped that Barnsley will long continue to remain a fitting memorial to a remarkable plantswomen.

Barnsley House

❊ CITY OF BATH BOTANICAL GARDENS

Some of the finest gardens within the Cotswolds are not located on large country estates, but within the boundaries of its towns and cities. Perhaps the most delightful of these is the Bath Botanical Gardens, which lie within Royal Victoria Park, just a stone's throw from Bath's famous Royal Crescent.

Royal Victoria Park was created in 1829 and was named in honour of Princess Victoria (then aged eleven) who was on her first visit to Bath at the time. Its 57 acres were originally laid out as an arboretum and still today contain an excellent collection of exotic trees and shrubs. In 1887, 9 acres of the park were turned into a botanic garden, the cost of which was funded by public subscription. Today this garden contains one of the most diverse collections of plants growing on limestone in south-west England. ▸

City of Bath Botanical Gardens

❋ CITY OF BATH BOTANICAL GARDENS

◄ Perhaps partly because of its early funding arrangements, this is by no means your typical botanic garden, full of scientifically arranged collections and labels; here aesthetics have always been uppermost in the minds of its curators and gardeners. There are numerous attractive and interesting features throughout the garden including a replica of the Roman Temple of Minerva, built for the British Empire Exhibition held at Wembley, London in 1924. Constructed of Bath stone, it was re-erected in the garden in 1926 where it stands proud above a pool and small cascade, both engulfed in a fecundity of foliage and flower.

From late spring to early autumn, one of the garden's most colourful features is a 70-metre-long (150 ft) border, filled with over 150 different herbaceous species and cultivars and always maintained to the highest standard. In early spring, a collection of magnolias takes centre stage, with many rare and beautiful species, such as *Magnolia dawsoniana* and *Magnolia liliiflora*, casting their sweet fragrance across drifts of narcissi and primula. In truth, this is a garden to visit at any time of the year such is the diversity of the collection – rock gardens, scented walks, a heather garden, the Great Dell full of gigantic American conifers and a butterfly garden all add to the delights of this splendid plant collection.

◄ Giant redwood sculpture

Replica of the Roman Temple of Minerva

❊ BATSFORD ARBORETUM

Batsford was originally designed and created in the late 1800s by Algernon Freeman Mitford – later Lord Redesdale – who, as a diplomat for the British Government, had spent much of his career working for the Foreign Office in China and Japan, where he fell in love with the plants and planting styles he encountered. During this time he became an accomplished plantsman and, in particular, an authority on bamboos. On his return to England in 1890 he began to create a wild garden with an oriental theme at his Batsford home in the Cotswolds. He imported bronze statues of Buddha, a Foo Dog and Japanese Sika Deer, planted hundreds of Asian trees and shrubs, built a life-size replica of a Japanese rest house, and created a 600-metre-long artificial stream, complete with pools, cascades and a Japanese-style bridge. All of this still exists today and the tree collection has developed into one of the finest in private hands. ▸

The Japanese bridge and stream   Early spring at Batsford Arboretum ▸

✤ BATSFORD ARBORETUM

◀ Batsford has a very different character to its larger arboreal Cotswold cousin at Westonbirt. In addition to the oriental influence, Batsford sits on a south-east-facing limestone escarpment with spectacular views towards the Cotswold town of Moreton-in-Marsh and the Evenlode valley beyond. The grounds, covering 20 hectares (50 acres), role gently down the slope – as does the original stream – bordered by great clumps of bamboo and frothy plantings of astibles, hostas and rodgersias. This sloping topography allows visitors the chance to get above the surrounding trees, providing opportunities to look down upon (or sometimes even meet at eye-level) such botanical delights as flowering magnolias, cherries and the amazing Pocket Handkerchief Tree.

Containing close on 100 different species of *Magnolia* and holding the National Collection (NCCPG) of Japanese Sato-Zakura village cherries, Batsford is a fine garden to visit in spring; however, autumn leaf colours in October can also be magnificent. Situated alongside the arboretum is the Batsford Falconry Centre with daily flying demonstrations.

Autumn tints and blue-needled cedars

❉ BERKELEY CASTLE GARDENS

Berkeley Castle is England's oldest inhabited castle. For over 800 years, twenty-four generations of the Berkeley family have lived here, transforming what was originally a formidable Norman fortress into a beautiful home and garden full of treasures.

The castle stands majestically upon an outcrop of red sandstone overlooking the Berkeley Vale and the River Severn beyond. Below and surrounding the castle, are a series of water-meadows which were originally used as part of the castle's defences. Criss-crossed by ditches, known as 'rheens', and controlled by a series of sluice gates, they could be flooded at will, thereby hindering the progress of any invading force. During the wet summer of 2007, these meadows were once again under water, as parts of Gloucestershire succumbed to the worst floods for sixty years.

The the early part of the twentieth century saw Gertrude Jekyll as a regular visitor to Berkeley, helping to design and plant up the terraces which climb from the meadows to the foot of the castle walls. She was undeniably moved by the romanticism of the location, as her writings at the time demonstrate: *'Seen from the meadows it looks like some great fortress roughly hewn out of natural rock. Nature would seem to have taken back to herself the masses of stone reared seven and a half centuries ago. The giant walls and mighty buttresses look as if they have been carved by wind and weather out of some solid rock-mass, rather than wrought by human handiwork. When the day is coming to its close and the light becomes a little dim, and thin mist-films arise from the meadows, it might be an enchanted castle, for in some tricks of evening light it cheats the eye into something ethereal, built up for the moment into towering masses of pearly vapour.'* ▶

The Lily Pond

◀ Today, these 'giant walls' are softened by a delightful collection of rare trees, shrubs and climbers, including two splendid examples of the Chinese *Magnolia delavayi*, which carry large creamy-white, fragrant flowers in summer, giant blue echiums from the Canary Islands, the South American climber *Solanum crispum*, a remarkable and formidable *Colletia paradoxa* with small white pitcher-shaped scented flowers, set amongst impenetrable triangular-shaped ferocious spines (surely the best defence for any castle wall), and, quite remarkably, a rampant *Caesalpinia pulcherrima* (Pride of Barbados), which has no right to be growing so vigorously this far north of the West Indies!

Elsewhere the terraces carry herbaceous borders, scented climbing roses, a lily pond (first built as a swimming pool), an Elizabethan grass bowling alley and a magnificent Scots Pine said to have been brought back as a pine cone from the Battle of Culloden by the 4th Earl of Berkeley in 1746.

◀ Berkeley's herbaceous borders

The Elizabethan grass bowling alley

✿ BLENHEIM PALACE

Containing some of the finest formal and Baroque-style gardens in Britain, the grounds of Blenheim Palace have long been a 'must see' for students of garden history and those who simply enjoy gardens with plenty of 'wow'! The scale and grandeur of both palace and garden lifts it into a class of its own and Blenheim's creator, Sir John Vanbrugh, along with the garden's architect, Archille Duchene, both considered Blenheim to be their greatest triumph, and rightly so. Here, water terraces, fountains, pools, statuary, swirling intricate box knots, flamboyant yew topiary, and a folly bridge with a main arch over 30 metres (100 feet) wide leave the visitor in no doubt that this really is gardening on the grandest of scales. Beyond the formal gardens, the parkland was the work of Lancelot 'Capability' Brown who scattered lakes, woodlands and vistas upon the landscape as if he were trying to compete with the great Creator himself.

There is, however, another side to Blenheim's gardens, a less formal and altogether more intimate affair, and one that perhaps relates more readily to our own gardens. Located roughly between the palace and the Pleasure Gardens is the 'Secret Garden'. It was originally laid out in the early 1950s by the respected nurseryman and plantsman Harold Hillier for the father of the present Duke of Marlborough, as his own private garden, and was deliberately designed to be in stark contrast to the wide, open grandeur of the overall Blenheim landscape. ▶

Blenheim Palace   Blenheim's magnificent Water Terraces ▶

✿ BLENHEIM PALACE

◀ Hillier had a reputation for planting rare and unusual trees and shrubs that had seldom been seen in British gardens before, and many were planted here at Blenheim as part of this new garden.

Neglected for over twenty-five years, it was restored in 2003 and today the Secret Garden is once again an absolute joy; an oasis of leafy informality, with looping paths, meandering stream, shady pools, waterfalls, and bridges, providing the backdrop to over 5,000 new plants complimenting those Hillier rarities that managed to survive the period of neglect. Emphasis is on foliage, interspersed with flower, bark and texture which, in combination, offer all-year-round attraction. Of particular note are fine collections of acer (Japanese maple) and dwarf conifer cultivars.

The Secret Garden

❋ BOURTON HOUSE GARDEN

Since receiving the prestigious HHA/ Christie's Garden of the Year Award in 2006, Bourton House Garden is no longer seen as 'just another garden' sandwiched between Batsford Arboretum and Sezincote. To be fair, it only occasionally was, but it is interesting to see how long it can sometimes take recent garden creations to receive the full recognition they deserve.

When Richard and Monique Paice arrived at Bourton House in 1983, they found a dilapidated house in need of tender, loving care and a 3-acre garden in a serious state of neglect. Over the last twenty-six years they and their team have peeled back those years of neglect, creating something quite

remarkable in the process. Without doubt, one of their finest creations is a box-edged parterre, inspired by a pattern from Chinese trellis furniture, with a raised stone pool at its heart and an ivy-clad arbour for those who wish to sit and reflect on this tranquil, green masterpiece. Elsewhere, box is used extremely effectively to provide low hedging for a small potager and a swirling knot garden by the main gates. Box buttresses and topiary spirals enhance the Cotswold-stone walls of the old kitchen garden and strong lines of stone-sided ponds, pools and fountains (each fed from clear Cotswold springs) are softened with box corners and margins. ▶

Central pool to the parterre

❀ BOURTON HOUSE GARDEN

◄ By contrast, a series of deep, herbaceous borders, surrounding and raised above an immaculate main lawn, introduce an exciting mix of colours, forms and textures to the garden. Here, thoughtfully chosen plants provide interest from early spring to the very end of autumn, and positioned on an eighteenth-century raised walkway at the far end of the lawn, a stone seat, set before a stained-glass window, overlooks both the garden and the rolling Cotswold landscape beyond.

Subtropical borders full of bananas, phormiums, cordylines and cannas, a wooden lathed shade house full of ferns and luxuriant foliage plants, a glasshouse of aeoniums, and a magnificent sixteenth-century tithe barn are just four more reasons why the gardens at Bourton House rank among the finest in the Cotswolds.

Sadly, during 2009 the gardens at Bourton House closed to visitors. At time of publication we are not sure when, or if, they will reopen.

◄ Box-edged parterre

Exciting mix of colours

❊ BUSCOT PARK

Buscot Park is an example of a garden that has evolved to absorb several influences and styles into one successful and quite beautiful landscape. Created between 1780 and 1783, the original grounds were laid out in the English landscape style and comprised 120 acres of deer park, 23 acres of plantations, 5 acres of lakes, 5 acres of walled kitchen gardens and 1 acre of ornamental shrubbery. In 1800, the estate was extended to include a further 107 acres, of which 20 acres formed a main lake positioned to the east of the house.

In 1904, Harold Ainsworth Peto, architect and garden designer with a great passion for Mediterranean architecture, was commissioned to create a link between the house and lake. He responded by building what is today regarded as one of the finest water gardens in Britain. It consists of a series of quatrefoil pools and rectangular basins, interlinked by a central canal complete with fountains, cascades and a beautiful Italianate bridge. Access down its length is by a series of stone stairways and the whole feature is bordered by formal lawns, statuary and fastigiate cypress trees, and enclosed within close-clipped box hedging. ▶

Borders designed by Peter Coates

The Peto Water Garden ▶

◀ Since 1978, the present Lord Faringdon has transformed the 5-acre walled kitchen garden into the Four Seasons Garden. Roughly octagonal in shape, the garden is intersected by two main axis paths that divide the whole into four quadrants. The east-west path is bordered by an avenue of pleached hop hornbeams *Ostrya carpinifolia* and the north-south path by Judas trees *Cercis silliquastrum*. Where these two paths intersect, there is a circular lily pool from which each of the four quadrants radiate. Each quadrant is planted to display colour, flower and foliage representative of one of the four seasons. Within each quadrant is a season-inspired classical statue designed by Frank Foster.

Elsewhere there are mirror borders of gold and purple foliage, designed and planted by Peter Coates, a delightful 'garden of swings' and a sunken amphitheatre full of potted citrus trees surrounding an Italian wellhead.

The Four Seasons Garden

❀ CERNEY HOUSE GARDENS

Situated just north of Cirencester, Cerney House has been the home of Sir Michael and Lady Angus since 1983. The house, which dates back to 1660, was extensively remodelled in both the Georgian and Victorian eras. The gardens are mainly situated to its rear where, in the bowl of a sheltered valley, there is a secluded, 3-acre, roughly rectangular, walled garden that is divided longitudinally into thirds. In Victorian times a third of the garden was an orchard, a third grew flowers and a third produced vegetables and fruit. Today, the south-facing slope is still given over to vegetables and the north-facing slope is still an orchard, but the central third has been turned into a delightful ornamental garden by Lady Angus and her daughter Barbara.

Immediately inside the garden a long grass avenue stretches ahead to steps and an opening in the far wall, beyond which is positioned an octagonal, open-fronted gazebo. Either side of the avenue are deep, colour-coordinated borders, full of hardy geraniums, paeonies, poppies, Lady's Mantle *Alchemilla mollis*, climbers such as *Clematis x durandii* and rambling roses galore, including Paul's Himalayan Musk, Seagull, Rambling Rector and the beautiful Veilchenblau. ▶

Cerney House in spring

◀ To the right of the avenue lies a knot garden. Cleverly concealed by a framework of climbers, it provides a sanctuary from the colours and busyness of the borders and a place to sit and relax. The knot is of common box *Buxus sempervirens* and has at its heart four quince trees *Cydonia oblonga*. The effect is quite magical and made more so by the planting within the knot itself, which is given over to magnificent displays of tulips in spring, but then left bare to accentuate the simplicity of the garden in summer.

A laburnum arch leads to a scented garden, beyond which lies the vegetable garden. Outside the walled garden are two well-labelled herb gardens, one containing culinary, and the other medicinal herbs. There is also a National Collection (NCCPG) of Tradescantia, an excellent collection of hardy geraniums, swathes of hellebores and snowdrops in early spring, and the ruins of an ancient chapel to explore and enjoy.

◀ Tulip displays in the walled garden

Quince trees in the knot garden

❀ COLESBOURNE PARK

In addition to being a plantsman of great repute, Henry John Elwes (1846-1922) was also a great traveller, exploring regions as diverse as Siberia, Taiwan, the Himalayas and the Andes. Along the way he introduced thirty-nine new plant species to Britain – ten of which bear his name. These plants, and thousands more collected on his travels, were planted at his family home, Colesbourne Park – which is situated roughly halfway between Cheltenham and Cirencester.

Elwes had a particular penchant for bulbs, including *Lilium*, *Nerine*, *Eremurus*, *Crocus*, *Fritillaria* and *Iris*. In the 1880s, his collection of bulbs at Colesbourne was described as being 'the finest collection in private hands'. One particular genus of bulb he cherished above all others was *Galanthus* and it is a snowdrop that has probably become one of his most lasting legacies. In April 1874, on a visit to western Turkey, he discovered a beautiful, large snowdrop in the mountains near Izmir. It was one of his finest plant discoveries and was latterly named *Galanthus elwesii* in his honour.

Following his death, the garden entered a period of steady decline, only to be rescued by his great-grandson – also Henry Elwes – and his wife Carolyn. ▸

Galanthus and *Crocus* at Colesbourne Park

Colesbourne's late summer borders ▸

◀ Together they have carefully nurtured the remains of the snowdrop collection; rediscovered specimens thought lost to the garden and planted many new species and cultivars. Today the snowdrop collection totals around 250 cultivars and species and is once again recognised as one of the finest gardens in Britain to view snowdrops.

Since 2003, new beds and borders of shrubs, herbaceous perennials and bulbs have been created to bring further interest into the garden in winter and spring.

Cyclamen, daphnes, viburnums, trilliums, helebores, cornus, candelabra primulas and golden-stemmed willows are all here in profusion, filling the garden with fragrance and colour.

In total, the garden covers 10 acres and includes an arboretum with fine specimen trees, such as Sargent's rowan *Sorbus sargentiana*, an old ice house, a delightful Cotswold church and a lake, the colour of which can only be described as intense, glacial blue.

Sargent's rowan *Sorbus sargentiana*

COTSWOLD WILDLIFE PARK

At first glance a wildlife park may not seem like an obvious place to find one of the Cotswolds' most exciting and innovative gardens, but do not be put off by the name, because what has long been a family favourite with animal lovers has, over the last few years, become an unexpected attraction for garden lovers, who revel in the rich diversity of plants and planting styles found throughout the 160 acres which surround the park's Regency Gothic manor house.

Herbaceous borders and formal parterres provide a well-maintained link with the past; however it is within the manor's original walled kitchen garden where the excitement really begins. Here, in what

Head Gardener Tim Miles describes as 'a theatre of plants', dramatic foliage and flower displays offer some hefty clues to a style of gardening that is likely to thrive in a climate-changing, global-warming UK.

Spiky-leaved palms, cordylines and yuccas, including the spectacular Californian 'Our Lord's Candle' *Yucca whipplei*, demonstrate just what can already be grown in a Cotswold garden. As with many supposedly tender exotic plants, yuccas can actually withstand several degrees of frost, however, it is wet soil conditions in winter that they cannot tolerate – which is why these particular arid beds are raised, sloping and covered with clinker to help maintain good drainage. ▸

Arid beds full of cactus and succulents

◀ This elaborate design was immortalised in a 1710 drawing by Johannes Kip. Although much had disappeared by the nineteenth century, in favour of an 'English landscape' with extensive parkland and trees (Repton visited the property in 1800), there are still glimpses of the original garden to be had today in the ponds and cascade on the west side of the house, the terrace and in the orangery, where fragrant citrus are grown much as in Blathwayt's time.

Today, the walk from the car park allows for appreciation of Dyrham's splendid 'natural' landscape, with far-reaching views towards the Bristol Channel and across extensive parkland dotted with groups of vast cedars, chestnuts and beech and grazed by herds of deer. The highlight of this walk is the sudden vista of the house and church, set amongst the surrounding hills. The statue of Neptune close by marks the spot where Blathwayt's original garden began. Behind and to the west of the house, the ornamental gardens include myrtles, magnolias, Indian bean trees *Catalpa bignonioides*, extensive borders and fine specimens of *Solanum crispum* 'Glasnevin' and *Actinidia kolomikta*.

◀ Extensive borders below the church

A glimpse of the original garden

❀ EASTLEACH HOUSE GARDENS

It is always pleasing to discover a garden which offers up more than your original expectation and one that deserves to be much better known than it is. The garden at Eastleach House is a perfect case in point. From the moment one ascends the steep winding gravel track to the house, passing beneath a majestic, old copper beech along the way, there is a sense of expectation and 'great things to come' and the garden, or, to be more accurate, gardens (for there are several), does not disappoint.

Stephanie Richards and her late husband David moved to the property in 1982, with the intention of creating a 'traditional English country garden' from scratch; and from scratch it most certainly was. The 1900s house stood on a hilltop surrounded by dense woodland, described by Stephanie as 'dark, forbidding wilderness'. There was no formal garden to speak of and most of the land beyond the wilderness was given over to horses and hens. ▸

The roundel with stag   The hidden Fountain Garden ▸

◀ Undaunted, she set about opening up the woodland to allow the light in, banished all livestock and then started on her grand design – although, in truth, there never was one – the garden evolved piece by piece, something you would never believe today. Over the last twenty-seven years and with no formal horticultural training, Stephanie has created a lime avenue with far-reaching vistas to the south across a central roundel (a rotunda without the dome cap) comprised of clipped yew encircling a magnificent statue of a stag, an arboretum full of interesting trees and shrubs, wildflower walks and a superb rill garden on a west-facing slope. Here, the use of plant colour, form and texture, in combination with a cascading rill made up of thirteen differing steps, makes for one of the best garden features in the Cotswolds. Of particular merit is an arc of silver-green stilted spheres of *Sorbus aria* 'Lutescens' set against a dark, evergreen backdrop.

To the north of the house a sunken woodland and wildlife garden has as its central feature a lily pool spanned by a 'Monet-esque' bridge draped with wisteria. The finest view of this exquisite scene is from a prospect window high above, reached by entering the irregular-shaped walled garden. Divided into five sections, the walled garden contains two knot gardens of box and a wonderful mix of flowering shrubs and scented perennials, interspersed with pergolas dripping with roses.

The Woodland and Wildlife Garden

❈ ERNEST WILSON MEMORIAL GARDEN

Question: what do the following plants all have in common? Regal lily, kiwi fruit, pocket-handkerchief tree, Chinese dogwood and the evergreen clematis *Clematis armandii*. Well in addition to being plants of great beauty, they are all plants introduced into cultivation by Ernest Wilson, one of the world's most esteemed plant collectors. Over the course of a plant hunting career which ran from 1899 to 1918, Wilson introduced over 1,000 new plant species into British gardens (mainly from China, Japan, Korea and Taiwan), many of which are considered today amongst our most cherished garden plants. Not only that, he was one of the very first botanists to record his finds using photography, compiling over 10,000 negatives and glass plates which showed not only plants, but the location they were discovered in too. During Wilson's career he was caught up in a landslide which broke his leg so badly that amputation was a serious consideration, almost drowned in rapids on the Yangtze River, and got involved in a Chinese armed rebellion. ▶

Entrance to The Ernest Wilson Memorial Garden

❀ ERNEST WILSON MEMORIAL GARDEN

◀ In 1984 a delightful commemorative garden, close to the Church in the centre of Chipping Campden, was officially opened by Roy Lancaster in memory of Wilson, who was born in the town in 1876. It consists solely of plants discovered or introduced by Wilson and includes primulas, poppies, roses, viburnums, magnolias and acers. Although less than an acre in size, it is an absolute delight and a place of great beauty and tranquillity, with plants such as the spectacular paper-bark maple *Acer griseum* ensuring that there is always colour and interest in the garden, even in the depths of winter. Meandering paths, pergolas and strategically placed seats make this a delightful place to linger and appreciate the accomplishments of this great man.

For a garden run on a volunteer basis, with no formal admission charge (donations gratefully received) the standard of horticultural maintenance is high, as is the plant labelling. Near the entrance, interpretation boards, describe Wilson's life and plant hunting expeditions and display several photographs from that era.

◀ Tibetan cherry *Prunus serrula*

Pocket-handerchief tree *Davidia involucrata*

❈ HIDCOTE MANOR GARDEN

Hidcote is without doubt one of the greatest English gardens created during the twentieth century. Not only that, it is also one of the most influential, having inspired generations of gardeners to design their own gardens as a series of outdoor 'rooms', each with its own style and individuality and separated from the whole by a series of hedges and walls. The fact that Hidcote predates Vita Sackville-West's famous White Garden at Sissinghurst is perhaps an indication as to just how influential this garden was.

Work began on the garden in 1907 when wealthy American socialite Gertrude Winthrop purchased the Hidcote Manor 280-acre estate and promptly handed it over to her son, Major Lawrence Waterbury Johnston. There is no evidence to suggest that either of them had created a garden before, but Johnston began work in earnest, initially planting shelter-belts of evergreen oak, to lessen the obvious climatic effects of Hidcote's exposed Cotswold position 200 metres (600 ft) above sea-level. Behind the oaks came hedges of box, yew, holly, beech and hornbeam. As they grew, they became increasingly clipped and shaped into intricate and architecturally pleasing 'walls' for Hidcote's twenty-two garden rooms. ▶

Mrs Winthrop's Garden

The Rose Walk ▶

❀ HIDCOTE MANOR GARDEN

◀ All part of a preconceived master design plan, or simply out of the necessity for shelter? In truth, we shall probably never know as there is little documentary evidence relating to this period. Either way, more than a century on from those humble beginnings, Hidcote is now firmly established as a jewel in the National Trust's crown (having been in their stewardship since 1948) and rightly so, for it is a garden of great beauty with ever-changing themes, reveals and vistas.

From the initial vista by the house, running away beneath a mature cedar tree and through the very heart of the garden to Heaven's Gate and the Cotswold escarpment beyond, this garden will tempt and entice you every step of the way.

One by one, the White Garden, the Maple Garden, the red borders, bright golden-yellow plantings of Mrs Winthrop's Garden, pools and streams, rose gardens, pavilions, topiary and stilted hornbeams, will assault your senses and leave you reeling with a hundred different images to take home and emulate in your own garden, or simply treasure as a memory of a wonderful day in a wonderful garden.

The Red Borders

❀ HUNTS COURT

Within a beautiful setting immediately below the western edge of the Cotswold escarpment, where the skyline is dominated by the splendid monument to William Tyndale (the first translator of the Bible into English), is Hunts Court, a delightful garden and a must for anyone who is interested in roses and, in particular, old, traditional roses. Here you will find species, climbers, shrub, albas, damasks, centifolias, gallicas and moss roses, in all numbering over 450 different varieties and complemented by over 500 other trees and shrubs, many of which are infrequently found within cultivation. If this were not enough, there are also considerable collections of hardy geraniums and penstemons.

The garden at Hunts Court, which is privately owned, has been developed since 1976 by Keith and Margaret Marshall, who were originally farmers before their love for ornamental plants and, in particular, roses took over. ▸

Blooms cascade in the Rose Walk

◀ Starting in the farmhouse garden, they quickly realised they needed more space and over the years since then have expanded into fields and orchards to both the north and south of the farmhouse drive, each time having to move the boundary fencing to allow for the expansion. What started off as just a quarter of an acre has now grown to almost three!

At its peak of flowering in late June, this is a wonderful garden with fragrant blooms cascading over arbours and pergolas and spilling from borders to fringe meandering grass paths. Hunts Court is, however, a garden to enjoy at other times of the year. There are fine collections of winter and spring flowering bulbs, shrubs and trees, and autumn colour is strong within the more recently created arboretum, where acers, cornus, cotinus and liquidambars abound. A nursery positioned alongside contains many of the plants seen in the garden.

In the words of Keith Marshall, '*Hunts Court Garden has been made by two people interested in plants, who also have the collectors touch of madness. At no time was Garden Design, with capital letters, on the agenda, we have simply chosen and placed plants where it is hoped they will look well and perhaps enhance their neighbours.*' Modest words indeed from someone who has created one of the loveliest gardens in the Cotswolds.

◀ The Shy Maiden

Roses in profusion

✽ IFORD MANOR – THE PETO GARDEN

This wonderful garden is just about as far south in the Cotswolds as you can go without falling off the edge into the Wiltshire/Somerset vale of the River Frome. However, its distance from the Cotswolds' 'tourism hotspots' of Burford, Bibury, Stow and Bourton is no reason at all for not visiting, because Iford is without doubt one of the finest gardens in the region and some would say the whole of England.

The manor house is built against the Cotswold escarpment with southerly views across the Frome. Immediately behind the house a series of spectacular garden terraces gently climb the hillside before gradually giving way to beech woodland. Iford was owned during the first part of the last century by Harold Peto, the much acclaimed architect and garden designer who taught Edwin Lutyens. Peto had a passion for classical Italian architecture and used this to great effect within many of his garden designs, including Ilnacullin in Ireland and Buscot Park in Oxfordshire; however, it was in his own garden at Iford that he truly reached his zenith. ▶

The Italian Colonnade

A series of terraces climb the hillside ▶

74

❀ IFORD MANOR – THE PETO GARDEN

◂ After several trips to Italy he had amassed a large collection of statuary and architectural fabric and by using this as his starting point, alongside Mediterranean plants such as Italian cypress and *Phillyrea*, he created a series of water features, pools, Italianate terraces and broad walkways, all bordered by great urns and colonnades and leading to intimate courtyards laid out in Romanesque style. The Casita and Cloister are two of the most beautiful garden buildings to be found outside Italy, and when they are cloaked in tumbling racemes of purple-pink wisteria flower the effect is truly sublime.

Overlooking all is a magnificent plane tree, casting shade and dappled light upon the terraces, just as it might in Sienna. Peto may have had a clear preference for structure, but his understanding and knowledge of plants is evident throughout the garden and they are thoughtfully used to both soften and enhance the architecture. Such is the dexterity with which this mix of formal and natural is applied, you could be forgiven for thinking the Cotswolds lay just down the road from Umbria!

The Casita Garden

❋ KELMSCOTT MANOR

Kelmscott Manor, situated close to the upper reaches of the River Thames, will forever be linked with one man – the poet, designer, socialist, and inspiration behind the Arts and Crafts Movement, William Morris. Kelmscott was his country home from 1871 until his death in 1896 and he loved it, describing it as a 'dear, sweet old place . . . having grown up out of the soil', 'a heaven on earth . . . and such a garden'. The garden delighted him as much as the house, enclosed by high walls and subdivided by dense hedges, it was his paradise away from the outside world. Not only that, the plants within it provided endless inspiration for his poetry, prose, textile patterns and wallpaper designs.

His letters refer to crocuses, aconites, '*snowdrops everywhere*', violets and primroses. May, his daughter, writes of the garden, '*gay with thousands of tulips*', '*the white foam of cherry blossom*' and the '*first purple-red rose*'.

After his death, members of Morris' family continued to live at Kelmscott until 1938, whereupon the estate was bequeathed to Oxford University. In 1962 the estate passed to the Society of Antiquaries of London and it is they who, in the mid 1990s, instigated a restoration of the garden, into something Morris would have recognised. Helping them in this work was a fine set of *Country Life* photographs taken in 1921. ▸

Morris' mulberry tree at the heart of the garden

◀ Today, the restoration reflects the rich botanical content of Morris' designs. There are once again wild tulips and snakeshead fritillaries under the original mulberry tree that Morris regularly sat beneath, herbaceous borders filled with hollyhocks, English cottage garden annuals, poppies, China asters, an orchard replanted with Victorian varieties and in the front garden, standard roses have been replanted to flank the path, as depicted in C. M. Gere's 1892 frontispiece to Morris's *News from Nowhere*. Close by, the original yew hedge had a topiary dragon clipped by Morris himself to represent 'Fafnir', the mythical dragon of his Icelandic poems. This has also been restored with the help of the National Trust. All in all, this is a remarkable garden restoration and one that will not only be of particular delight to followers of Morris, but relished by anyone who has an eye for a beautiful garden.

◀ Kelmscot Manor   Fruit and flowers reflect Morris' designs

✤ KEMPSFORD MANOR

This beautiful garden, which has changed little in fifty years, retains an air of timeless charm. From the terrace in front of the 300-year-old manor house – normally full to overflowing with substantial pots of old-variety geraniums – there are superb views across a rectangular, sunken rose garden with a circular lily pool at its centre, towards two magnificent, deep herbaceous borders beyond. The emphasis in the borders is on bright summer colour and flame-orange crocosmias, golden-yellow rudbeckias and bold clumps of acanthus intermingle with lilac sedums, large white daisies and purple asters; whilst earlier in the year, delphiniums, lupins and poppies all jostle for position.

The borders are bisected by a grass path that runs away from the house towards a coyly clad female statue sheltering beneath a majestic pine (undoubtedly more than fifty years old) in the distance. To one side lies a croquet lawn, beyond which there are several young specimen trees including birch, beech, *Zelkova* and a particularly fine specimen of Lebanon cedar. ▸

Terraces overflowing with geraniums

Herbaceous borders across the lily pool ▸

❃ KEMPSFORD MANOR

◀ Beyond the trees, but still on manor land – which in total amounts to seven acres (2.8 hectares) – lies the Kempsford cricket pitch. Visitors to the garden (or those taking advantage of the thriving bed and breakfast which the manor offers) are able to sit on a seat in the garden and watch this most English of games played within one of the most English of landscapes.

To the far side of the cricket pitch a line of poplars and aspens denotes a walk that follows the route of the old Thames & Severn Canal. Along the walk you can clearly see the original towpath and both sides of the canal. Given recent plans to restore the canal, it may not be too long before barges will once again be seen passing by just beyond the boundary rope.

The canal walk leads to the manor's vegetable garden and then into an orchard of traditional apple, pear and plum trees.

Kempsford Manor

❀ KIFTSGATE COURT GARDEN

Ask most gardeners what the name 'Kiftsgate' brings to mind and you will probably be told a rose – a very vigorous rose. For 'Kiftsgate' is a named cultivar of *Rosa filipes*, an aggressive but deliciously scented rambling rose, first named at Kiftsgate Court in 1951. However, Kiftsgate is far more than just one rose, it is a remarkable garden, created, developed and maintained by three generations of lady gardeners from the same family.

Heather Muir began work on the garden in 1920, creating a whole series of gardens and borders around the house, within which she paid particular attention to colour. Her feel for colour combinations was undoubtedly first class and by the 1950s Kiftsgate was a garden of much repute. '*I regard this garden as the finest piece of skilled colour work that it has been my pleasure to see,*' wrote Graham Scott Thomas in the *RHS Journal*.

In 1954, daughter Diany Binny took up the baton and, after an initial reluctance to alter her mother's designs, gradually began to add to, rather than change, the original garden. ▸

Colour combinations at their best

❁ KIFTSGATE COURT GARDEN

First came a semi-circular plunge pool, laid out on a terrace below a steep west-facing bank, upon which she bestowed woody plants and climbers. In 1972 a further pool, complete with fountain (inspired by a visit to the Chelsea Flower Show), was added to the centre of the white sunken garden.

By 1981, her daughter Anne and husband Johnny Chambers were becoming increasingly immersed in the garden. During their tenure they have developed extensive gardens of tender plants on the sheltered west-facing bank, created a wonderful 'Millennium' water garden and continue to maintain, enrich, and indeed enhance the plantings within the original borders.

Today, the garden bears witness to a family blessed with three generations of remarkable gardeners. Besides the obvious continuity, there is a feeling of contentment, timelessness, indeed tranquillity, which settles over you within moments of entering the garden. It is a garden which is at peace with itself, where nothing jars the eye and yet the senses are set tingling by so much colour and fragrance.

◀ The west-facing slope below the Court

The Millennium Water Garden

✤ THE MATARA GARDENS

Otherwise know as the meditative garden, this intriguing landscape is full of magical and spiritual symbolism but manages to combine it with good horticulture. At its centre is a garden inspired by the great Scholar's Gardens of China. These gardens originally developed from the belief that contemplation of natural landscapes – mountains, lakes, plants, etc. – leads to human fulfilment. Given that it is not always possible to be amongst such landscapes, skilled Chinese designers, over a period lasting more than 500 years, created many representations of natural landscapes on a garden scale, using pools for lakes, carefully selecting and placing rocks for mountains and plants indigenous to these areas but restricted in their growth and habit (penjing) – a technique which both preceded and inspired Japanese bonsai. Within these gardens, architecture was introduced in the form of pavilions or rest houses, intended as places to both view and reflect on the garden, quite often through ornamental 'prospect windows'. ▶

The Prospect Moongate

Matara's Chinese Garden ▶

❂ THE MATARA GARDENS

◀ There are few such gardens in Britain, but here at Matara one has been skilfully created, providing a worthy glimpse of this delightful garden style, and whether you are open to meditation or not, I guarantee that once there you will want to take 'time out' to reflect on its beauty.

Despite its uniqueness, it would be wrong of me to dwell on just this one feature within Matara's landscape, for there is more to this garden. Beyond a traditional Japanese *Shinto torii* wooden archway, woodland of beech, hazel and yew has been augmented with *Shinto*-inspired natural sculptures alongside brightly coloured wishing ribbons attached to evergreen foliage. Elsewhere, a stone labyrinth and spiral maze will lead both you and your mind away from the stresses and strains of everyday life, whilst cascades and ponds offer further opportunities for quiet contemplation. An ornamental vegetable garden, bordered by box hedging, has a small fountain at its centre, and close to the Matara Centre there are further courtyard gardens to explore and even a Chinese-inspired zigzag bridge – useful when warding off evil spirits, as apparently they can only travel in straight lines.

Pastel shades in the Walled Garden

❀ MILL DENE GARDEN

This delightful garden, created by owners Barry and Wendy Dare in the village of Blockley, 3 miles west of Moreton-in-Marsh, is a wonderful mix of Cotswold cottage garden sobriety and quirky surprises inspired by Wendy's rather keen sense of humour. The name 'Dene' means wooded valley and the Dare's property is one of twelve mills within the Blockley valley mentioned in the Domesday Book of 1086. Theirs was originally a flour mill, becoming, over the next 700 years, a wool mill and a silk mill.

The lower parts of the garden are set around the millpond, race and stream, above which a series of terraces climbs quickly up both the north-facing and south-facing slopes of the valley. Alongside the cool and shaded millstream there is a beautiful stone grotto, decorated in swirling patterns of mussel and scallop shells and set amongst classical architectural relics and striking foliage plants, such as Brazilian rhubarb *Gunnera manicata*, skunk cabbage *Lysichiton americanum* and tree ferns *Dicksonia antarctica*. ▶

A cottage garden delight

❈ MILL DENE GARDEN

◀ Higher up, on the south-facing terraces – interlinked by curving stone steps fringed with dwarf cotoneaster – there are rose walks, fruit gardens, herbaceous borders and a beautifully designed potager full of culinary and medicinal plants, alongside which a babbling rill and water feature flow.

It is this great diversity that gives Mill Dene both its interest and horticultural strength, making it feel, in the process, far larger than its two-and-a-half acres, an effect which is further enhanced by the clever use of 'borrowed landscape' in several places.

Look out for the cricket lawn complete with wicket and an old summerhouse lovingly transformed into a cricket pavilion, above which the flag of St George gently flutters. Yes, this is England at its best and will probably bring a tear to the eye of any lover of the game who sits on one of the white wooden benches (that once had pride of place in the Mound Stand at Lord's) to admire the garden.

Mill Dene is undoubtedly a garden of great warmth and charm. Visit once and I guarantee you will want to return.

◀ From Lord's to the Lords's House

Water plays a big part in this garden

❋ MISARDEN PARK

This lovely, unspoilt garden, positioned high on the Wolds and commanding spectacular views across Misarden deer park to extensive woodland beyond, was created in the seventeenth century and still retains a wonderful sense of timeless peace and tranquillity. Much of the original garden is found within ancient Cotswold-stone walls, which are at one point completely engulfed by the Tolkien-like roots of a remarkable sycamore tree. Extensive yew hedging bisects the garden and creates a notable yew walk in the process. To one side of the walk a parterre, with a sundial at its centre, is planted with a selection of potentilla, lavender and allium. The predominate colours of silver, grey, blue and pink contrast well with a rose-clad arbour alongside, which provides welcome shade in high summer.

Perhaps the finest features in the garden are two double mixed borders which have undergone a total replant in recent years and now contain a wide range of roses, clematis, shrubs and herbaceous plantings, all arranged in individual colour sections and cleverly designed to provide flower and interest from spring until autumn. ▶

Springtime in Misarden Park

Misarden's recently restored herbaceous borders ▶

◀ Directly below the lodge a series of cliff walks (reputedly laid out with the help of Gertrude Jekyll) wind their way down the escarpment to the remains of pleasure grounds created in the late eighteenth century. Here, there is an ornamental carp pond, partially enclosed by a south-facing crinkle-crankle serpentine wall, the bays of which would at one time have been used for growing fruit. At the eastern end of the wall is a summerhouse, which has been restored since the property was given to the National Trust in 1949.

Much of the credit for the restoration work that has taken place at Newark Park must go to Robert Parsons, who was the property tenant for thirty years from 1970 until his death in 2000. Assisted by Michael Claydon (who is continuing this work with the support of the Trust), they not only helped to bring the original property back to life, but developed several new garden features along the way, including a walled garden to the eastern end of the lodge and a Peafowl House which provides a delightful focal point at the end of the south terrace.

◀ The Peafowl House

Ornamental carp pond and summerhouse

✿ OWLPEN MANOR

'Owlpen – Ah, what a dream is there!' So said Vita Sackville-West, following a visit to Owlpen Manor in 1941. Almost seventy years on, Owlpen still portrays a sense of timeless beauty and tranquillity that is positively dream-like. Not only that, it is set in one of the loveliest locations in England, nestling as it does, deep within a wooded combe on the very edge of the Cotswold escarpment with wonderful views of the surrounding hills rolling gently away to the distant plains of the Severn Valley.

The name 'Owlpen' derives from the name for a local Saxon chieftain known as Olla. It was he who first set up a 'pen' (an enclosure for containing stock) in the valley in the ninth century. The origins of the present manor date back to 1450 and only minor alterations have been made to the house since 1616. It is a fascinating building and visitors are welcome, indeed encouraged, to explore its interior, even though it is still a family home for Karin and Nicholas Mander. ▶

Parterre of box and yew

'One of the loveliest locations in England' ▶

◀ The Manders arrived in 1974 and have lovingly cared for both the manor and its gardens ever since.

Like the manor, the garden has changed very little in 400 years. The overall structure of terracing, paths, vistas and main garden axis, were all laid out during the Tudor period. The whole is enclosed by Cotswold-stone walls and yew hedging, creating the feel of a fortified courtyard. In the centre, a parterre of close clipped box and yew surrounds a circular pool and beds planted with Narcissi, tulips, fritillaries and alliums.

One of Owlpen's finest features is a rectangular 'room' made entirely of yew, the walls of which are at least 6 metres (20 feet) high and 1 metre (3 feet) wide. Known today as the 'Yew Parlour', this amazing creation, used in the past to stage dances and other forms of entertainment, was designed and planted by Thomas Daunt in the 1720s.

Recent features include lines of pleached hornbeam and lime and a delightful stilted allée of Portuguese laurel orbs.

Pleached hornbeam and laurel orbs

❀ OZLEWORTH PARK

Whatever I say about this stunning garden (which opens to the public on specific charity days each year), it will not be enough to do justice to the astonishing transformation which has taken place here since I first stumbled across the property in the early 1990s. Back then the house was empty and its once-great garden completely neglected. Inside the walled garden, rotting greenhouses were falling off the walls, and the nineteenth-century bathhouse was quite simply a mud-filled health and safety nightmare. Gazing sadly down on this forgotten landscape were three Lebanon cedars, full of deadwood but somehow offering just a hint of past glory. In truth, the only part of the landscape which seemed to have escaped the ravages of time was the Norman-towered church with circular walled churchyard, which stood – and still stands – at the very centre of the property. ▶

The Norman-towered church at the centre of the property

◀ By the end of the twentieth century, however, Ozleworth was under new ownership, with a new head gardener installed and the work of restoration had begun. Restoration is perhaps the wrong word, because alongside the original garden's renovation many new and exciting features have also been created, helping to make this twelve-acre garden, today, one of the finest jewels in the Cotswolds' horticultural crown.

The garden is normally open for charity in July, which no doubt reflects the wealth of roses to be found here, however, that is only part of the story. Deep colour-coordinated herbaceous borders line the path to the bathhouse, which now holds crystal-clear spring waters that offer looking-glass reflections of the 'classical' mural on its circular walls. An espaliered pear pergola underplanted with agapanthus and alliums, leads to the extensive fruit, vegetable and flower-cutting gardens, beyond which twenty-first century glasshouses boast peaches and grapes by the bucket-full.

One of the highlights of Ozleworth is undoubtedly the terraced rill garden. Bordered by walnut trees and fringed by marginal bog and foliage plants, it gracefully ascends an escarpment whilst gradually moving from formality to wilderness – masterful in its execution and a place to linger and reflect on the changing fortunes of this remarkable garden.

◀ A wealth of roses

Herbaceous borders line the path to the bath house

❋ PAINSWICK ROCOCO GARDEN

Mention Painswick Rococo Garden in a crowded room and I guarantee one of the first responses will include a reference to snowdrops. Whilst this is in some ways understandable, given that the garden boasts one of the best displays of this indomitable herald of spring, there is a real danger that a strong association such as this may act as a barrier to fully experiencing and enjoying just what this remarkable garden has to offer outside of January and February.

Rococo refers to a brief period in garden history from around 1720 to 1760 when gardens were beginning to shake off the sobriety and formality of the seventeenth century, but had not quite made it to the gloriously unshackled picturesque landscape movement, which – through the introduction of the ha-ha by Charles Bridgeman – allowed garden designers such as William Kent and 'Capability' Brown to embrace the wider countryside whilst blurring the edges of the garden boundary. ▸

The Red House

The Exedra ▸

✤ PAINSWICK ROCOCO GARDEN

◀ Rococo gardens, like Painswick, were asymmetrical, full of flamboyant, even quirky architecture, which quite often served no other purpose than to amuse and delight. However, rather like the 'roaring twenties' or the 'swinging sixties' following on from the austerity of the post-war years of the twentieth century, the Rococo candle burned bright but was quickly extinguished. By the end of the eighteenth century, few gardens of this style remained.

Painswick's layout was changed and the garden eventually abandoned but never completely destroyed. Then, in 1976, an exhibition of paintings by Thomas Robins revealed a detailed canvas of Painswick Rococo Garden, painted when the garden was at its peak in 1748. By 1984, a restoration project had begun, using the painting as a blueprint for returning Painswick's overgrown wilderness to its eighteenth-century glory.

Today, this fascinating 6-acre garden restoration is nearing completion and comprises a series of delightful follies, each with dramatic vistas across the garden, plunge pools, ponds, old-fashioned herbaceous borders, a tunnel arbour of hornbeam, large kitchen garden, and a privet maze planted in 1998 to celebrate the 250th anniversary of the Thomas Robins painting.

You may have enjoyed the snowdrops – now go and enjoy the rest!

The Eagle House

✤ PRIOR PARK LANDSCAPE GARDEN

The Palladian bridge in Prior Park just outside Bath is one of the most photographed architectural features in any Cotswold landscape. Built in 1755 by Richard Jones for Prior Park owner Ralph Allen, it is one of the best examples in Britain of the Palladian style of architecture as practised by the Italian architect Andrea Palladio (1508-80).

Simply to view the bridge is reason enough to visit Prior Park; however, there is far more to this magnificent landscape. The Palladian bridge was in fact just one feature in a garden landscape designed to do justice to Allen's splendid Palladian mansion, built at the head of a small, steep valley overlooking the Bath skyline.

In all, the garden took almost thirty years to create. Over this period its development fell into three distinct phases. The first, saw the laying out of the general shape of the grounds with some areas of formal planting and a contrived 'wilderness' of trees and shrubs, within which were placed a grotto, a serpentine lake and water cascade, a grass cabinet (a roughly circular, open area where people congregated and performances were staged), and a sham bridge. ▸

Prior Park Landscape Garden

✿ PRIOR PARK LANDSCAPE GARDEN

◀ The second phase saw the creation of a larger cascade positioned down the centre of the valley, and the enlargement of old ponds, one of which was then crossed by the Palladian bridge.

The third and final phase of the development saw the involvement of Lancelot 'Capability' Brown, who removed the central cascade and replaced it with a sweep of grassland linking the mansion at the top of the valley with the Palladian bridge at the bottom. Finally, Brown softened the edges of the tree and shrub plantings to help draw the eye down the length of the valley.

Standing today at the head of the valley immediately below the mansion – now Prior Park College – the view down to the Palladian bridge and the Bath skyline beyond is breathtaking and all credit must be given to the National Trust for their faithful (and ongoing) restoration of the serpentine lake, the water cascade, the cabinet, and other garden infrastructure.

◀ The Palladian Bridge

Across the landscape to the Bath skyline beyond

❋ RODMARTON MANOR

To the west of Cirencester lies what is believed to be one of the last great manor houses to have been built in the Cotswolds – Rodmarton Manor. Created for the Biddulph family between 1909 and 1926, both house and garden are a shining example of the work undertaken by the Cotswold Arts and Crafts Movement, led by Ernest Barnsley and inspired by William Morris.

The gardens were designed and constructed to be at one with the house.

Each window of the house looks out onto a garden 'room' specifically designed for the purpose and from each garden the reverse applies as varying elevations of the house are revealed. The immediate garden 'rooms' are relatively formal, becoming less so with greater distance from the house, until finally they relax into an informality that leads seamlessly into the wider Cotswold landscape and eventually offers up far-reaching views to the Marlborough Downs. ▶

The Box Topiary Garden

Rodmarton's 'crowning glory' ▶

◀ There are eighteen different 'rooms' in total, and a tour of the garden is truly a journey of discovery, as rooms and features reveal themselves one by one.

Some of the finest features are to be found close to the house, including a tightly pleached structure of lime trees with a summer latticework canopy of foliage and sculptural heads of crimson shoots in winter. The symmetry of the nearby box topiary garden is simply stunning, as is the delightful 'Troughery' where twenty ancient stone troughs, each carved from individual blocks of Cotswold limestone, have been accumulated from all corners of the Rodmarton estate and carefully filled with a variety of alpines, creating tiny rock gardens of exquisite beauty.

Rodmarton's crowning glory is probably its herbaceous borders. There are four in total, two either side of a deep, crystal-clear pool. They run in an east-west direction with the house at the easterly end and a beautiful summerhouse to the west. Surrounded by thick, close-clipped yew hedging, which both shelters and provides a dark foil for the flowering colour spectrum within, they guarantee spectacular displays all summer long.

The Summerhouse

✤ ROUSHAM PARK

It is not very often that one has the opportunity to visit a garden which is pretty much as it was when created. Normally, time clothes the original concept; either in layers of neglect, or layers of 'improvements' carried out by successive generations of zealous owners and head gardeners. Not so at Rousham, situated north of Oxford in the rolling Oxfordshire Cotswolds. Here, today, is a garden which would be instantly recognisable to its creator, William Kent, despite the fact that over 270 years have passed since he drew up the plan for the garden in 1738.

Not only that, Rousham has managed to maintain an air of unspoilt simplicity in an age when properties open to the public are under ever-increasing pressure to develop shops, cafés, garden centres and an events programme as long as your arm!

Rousham is a supreme example of the first phase in English landscape design, that joyous period following Charles Bridgeman's invention of the ha-ha, which, at a stroke, swept away formal barriers needed to separate garden from grazing animals and the wider landscape beyond. ▸

The Praeneste

◀ This in turn led to a softer, more picturesque and naturalistic interpretation of garden design, which embraced the surrounding countryside, using it firstly as a backdrop to the garden, but then as an integral part of the garden itself.

At Rousham, Kent's garden utilises natural slopes, hills and vistas, sprinkled with lakes, pools, serpentine rills and classical architectural features such as Doric temples and Greek mythological statues, all set against a foil of dark-green box and yew foliage. Perhaps the finest feature of all is the Praeneste, a superb seven-arched arcade, designed in classical style and formed against the hill.

In all, there are 25 acres of landscape gardens to enjoy, plus a walled garden of true beauty and tranquillity. Here you will find a magnificent herbaceous border, which runs along the entire length of the north-facing wall, a pergola dripping with old-fashioned roses, vines and wisteria, a circular pool with a fountain, and a pigeon cote built in 1685 and still containing its original revolving ladder.

◀ The Doric Temple

Pigeon Cote in the Walled Garden

❀ RUSKIN MILL

At first glance, connoisseurs of gardens may well ask why the gardens at Ruskin Mill, located in a steep-sided, wooded valley, close to the Cotswold town of Nailsworth, are included in a book such as this. After all, they are not listed, historic, created by a well-known garden designer, or full of rare and beautiful plants. My answer to this is simple: gardens are about people just as much as plants. People influence the style and make-up of a garden landscape, and in return, people are influenced by the gardens they work and walk in. The gardens at Ruskin Mill are a perfect example as to how we can be positively influenced by a garden and the actual process of gardening.

Originally a sixteenth-century watermill used for working corn and then as a textile mill, Ruskin Mill today still retains its waterwheel, millpond and race. However, in 1967, the mill was more or less derelict when Robin and Barbara Gordon moved there with their two sons, Aonghus and Alasdair. Inspired by the work of William Morris, John Ruskin and Rudolf Steiner, by 1984 they had turned the property into the Ruskin Mill Centre for Arts and Cultural Regeneration, working along the way with students from the nearby Cotswold Chine Special School. ▶

Horsley Mill at Ruskin Mill (Photo by Howie Russell)

High summer in the valley ▶

◀ Aonghus Gordon discovered that when students with learning difficulties, or those who, for whatever reason, had fallen between the cracks of mainstream educational provision, worked in natural environments on real-life, purposeful tasks, such as horticulture, their personal, emotional and social skills, behaviour and health, improved dramatically.

Today, Ruskin Mill offers places to around 100 students between the ages of sixteen and twenty-four, who spend anything up to three years following a vocational curriculum, specifically designed to meet their individual needs. They leave feeling good about life and themselves, and I guarantee, when you leave after a visit, you too will feel the same.

Permissive paths lead past herbaceous borders, waterside plantings, lily ponds, swathes of prairie-style grassland, herbs, productive vegetable plots, orchards, beehives, hazel coppice and sculptures, all set to a backdrop of millpond and woodland. But do not go expecting it to be manicured and prissy; this is very much a working garden and, in my opinion, all the better for that.

An intimate mix of flowers and vegetables

❋ SEZINCOTE

Few Cotswold garden properties are more indicative of another world than Sezincote. Quite often described as 'India in the Cotswolds', its design is based upon the work of the sixteenth to eighteenth-century Mughal rulers of India, and is therefore predominantly Islamic and Persian in origin, rather than Indian Hindu. However, it is difficult not to bring the subcontinent to mind as you wander through its evocative landscapes.

Architect Samuel Cockerell and the artist Thomas Daniell, both of whom spent many years working in India, created house and garden from 1805 to 1807, and it is reputed to have been the inspiration for the Brighton Pavilion. One of the great features of the house is the magnificent 'onion dome' which floats ethereally above the roof. Originally burnished copper, now dressed in a blue-green coat of verdigris, it is typically Muslim and represents heart and heaven – a symbol of peace and tranquillity. ▸

Sezincote Orangery

◀ Ironically, one of the great features of the garden owes nothing to either Cockerell or Daniell and was created by Lady Kleinwort (with the help of Graham Stuart Thomas), following her visit to India in 1965. It is based on a design for the traditional 'Paradise Garden' and includes a formal canal bordered by spire-like conifers and crossed at its centre point by a path, thereby symbolising the four rivers of life. A pool at its heart represents the coming together of God and Man. The garden is formal and tranquil, simple but complex, and reminiscent of the garden leading to the Taj Mahal.

Bordering the western extremity of the Paradise Garden is an orangery bedecked with chattris (small minarets) and housing several citrus trees and tender shrubs and climbers, including a rampant double yellow Banksian rose, an intensely scented Chinese jasmine and two container grown specimens of *Michelia figo*, the flowers of which emit a delicious aroma of ripe bananas and pear drops!

To the north of the house an informal water garden, made up of a series of still pools, sparkling fountains and cascades, tumbles through streamside plantings of hostas, astibles, rodgersias, skunk cabbage *Lysichiton americanum* and *Iris pseudacorus*. Here too, the Indian theme continues with a small temple dedicated to the Hindu sun god, Surya, and an Indian bridge bedecked with Brahmin bulls.

A frequent visitor to Sezincote in the 1920s was Sir John Betjeman, who loved the property and immortalised it within his poem, 'Summoned by Bells'.

◀ Persian-inspired architecture   Temple dedicated to the Hindu sun god, Surya

✤ SNOWSHILL MANOR

Snowshill Manor is situated high on a Cotswold escarpment with far-reaching views to the Vale of Evesham. Part of the manor house, which is built of local stone the colour of honeycomb, dates back to the early 1500s. It was originally owned by the Abbey of Winchcombe, until the dissolution of the monasteries in 1539, and since then has seen many alterations and additions, with perhaps the most dramatic changes taking place from 1919, when Charles Paget Wade, a sugar plantation owner, purchased the property and began a process of restoration and renewal.

Wade, an advocate of the Arts and Crafts Movement, intended to use the manor to display his ever-growing collection of crafts and eclectic artefacts. In 1920, he commissioned the Arts and Crafts architect M. H. Baillie-Scott to produce a design for the garden that would transform what Wade considered at the time to be a 'wilderness of chaos' sloping steeply away from the house. Over the next three years, this 'wilderness' was levelled and terraced and then turned into a series of charming interconnecting 'garden rooms', which took in several old farm buildings and a seventeenth-century dovecot. ▸

The garden comprises a series of interconnecting 'garden rooms'

Through the garden gate ▸

❈ SNOWSHILL MANOR

◀ Today these rooms, separated by Cotswold-stone walling bedecked in climbing roses, clematis and honeysuckle, make for a wonderful journey of discovery. Each area displays its own character and theme, some formal, some informal. Features include a sunken lily pool, herbaceous borders brimming with shades of blue, mauve and lilac, manicured lawns, stone-flag terraces, a number of small, trickling water features – the sound of which echoes around the walls – and several exquisitely produced examples of Arts and Crafts work, ranging from clocks to lattice-work windows. Woodwork throughout the garden is painted 'Wade blue', a powder-blue colour which offsets the Cotswold stonework beautifully. One of Snowshill's particular delights is the succession of vistas that open up through gateways and windows as you circumnavigate the garden. Beyond the outdoor rooms there are further gardens including colourful flower borders, a productive vegetable garden and an orchard.

In 1951 Charles Paget Wade gave the manor and its contents to the National Trust, who continue to manage the property to this day. Since 1990, the garden has been run on organic principles.

Snowshill Manor positioned high on a Cotswold escarpment

❄ STANCOMBE PARK

Essential ingredients needed to make any garden inspirational are successful planting schemes, well-designed infrastructure, strong vistas, and atmosphere. The latter does not necessarily stem from the previous three and without it, a garden will never – in my opinion – become truly inspirational. Stancombe Park has atmosphere by the bucket-load, plus all the other essential ingredients, and is, therefore, one of the most inspirational gardens in the Cotswolds.

Stancombe's main historical garden is the Folly Garden, occasionally referred to as Victorian Gothic in design. This is something which sends owner Mrs Gerda Barlow into a frenzy of indignation, and, of course, she is right, because the Folly Garden originates from around 1820, seventeen years before Victoria came to the throne. It was created by Bransby Purnell, who used the labour of soldiers returning from the Napoleonic wars. Nor is it Gothic; taking its influence not from the mediaeval period but from classical Greek mythology and ancient Egypt. ▶

The Temple

◀ In a steep-sided wooded combe, hidden from the house and approached via a narrow, shrub-lined walkway, Purnell created an enchanting landscape of lakes, streams, grottos, Egyptian tombs, dark tunnels guarded by huge stone dogs – like Cerberus guarding Hades – and a beautiful Doric Temple. Elsewhere there are Chinese pavilions with original lead glazing, fountains, vine-covered pergolas and Roman mosaic. Almost 200 years later and despite its genteel decay, Purnell would still recognise his landscape and it is this decaying splendour which gives Stancombe its atmosphere. Even the newly built Millennium Folly, erected at the head of Middle Lake, has reused the façade of a ruined chapel discovered deep in the woods.

Since 1964, several new gardens have been created close to the house by Gerda and Basil Barlow and designer Nada Jennett. Here, close-clipped yew and box hedging flows through four borders, providing a strong pattern for informal plant compositions of silver, gold and blue. Beyond, a fine, pleached lime-walk leads from a seat surrounded by cherubs to a large Italian urn encircled by golden-leaved maples.

◀ View to the Chinese Pavilion

Borders created since 1964

❊ STANWAY HOUSE

Once called 'as perfect and pretty a Cotswold manor house as anyone is likely to see', Stanway House has a sublime beauty which is matched only by the tranquillity of its surroundings, and for that alone it deserves its place on the 'must visit' list for those exploring the Cotswolds. There is, however, another reason for its continuing popularity; the introduction in 2004 of a new 'water feature' in the garden. Now, there are water features and water features; however, the one at Stanway is, quite simply, in a class of its own. Named the High Fountain, it sends a single jet of water almost 100 metres (300 feet) into the air, and as such is the highest gravity fountain in the world. The resulting shimmering curtain of falling water is visible over a mile away and on sunny days carries with it a multitude of rainbows.

Stanway has a long association with water. In the 1720s, a magnificent water garden was created on the slopes of the steep Cotswold escarpment that rises to the east of the Jacobean manor house. Most probably designed by Charles Bridgeman, who was the catalyst for the English landscape garden movement, it comprised a single pyramid, from which a 190-metre-long cascade descended into a grand canal on the terrace immediately above the house. ▸

Stanway House

The High Fountain ▸

◂ There was a further cascade and pond to the east of the pyramid and a tufa waterfall. Sadly, over time, much of the garden fell into disrepair and was eventually lost to view. However, in 1986 work began to identify the exact positioning of the original features. Restoration of the canal took place in 1998 and since then the pyramid pond and a short section of the cascade have also been restored. It is in the canal that the High Fountain now stands.

Given the space I have devoted to the Water Garden, you could be forgiven for thinking there is little else to see at Stanway, but that is far from true. In the Lower Garden, outside the magnificent fourteenth-century tithe barn, is a restored mediaeval pond fringed with ornamental trees and shrubs. Close by is a delightful walled garden containing pergolas clothed in roses and clematis, a lily pond, productive vegetable garden and a nursery full of young lime trees *Tilia* sp., which will eventually become new avenues of lime striding across Stanway's 400-acre parkland.

The Pyramid

❈ STONE HOUSE GARDEN

Wyck Rissington lies just a stone's throw from Bourton-on-the-Water. It has a timeless unspoilt charm, a large village green, a village pond with original 'slipway' to allow access for livestock, and a Norman square-towered church, where the composer Gustav Holst used to play the organ. It also has the added bonus of the delightful garden at Stone House, a Cotswold property on the edge of the village. The garden is relatively new, having been designed and created, more or less from scratch, by owners Katie Lukas and her husband Andrew over the last seventeen years. However, there is nothing adolescent about this garden, indeed the surprise is just how quickly it has reached a good degree of maturity.

The garden is made up of a series of outdoor 'rooms' with each room flowing seamlessly into the next, offering teases of what is to come through windows cut through foliage and the clever use of meandering paths. Particularly successful is the way the garden does not amputate itself from the surrounding countryside. At several locations, vistas lead the eye from the garden, across the surrounding paddocks grazed by rare-breed sheep, to the misty-blue outline of the Cotswold hills beyond. ▸

Windows cut through foliage offer teases

✿ STONE HOUSE GARDEN

◀ A touch of pure genius is to be found on the edge of the ha-ha where two slate-blue urns reflect the same colouring back into the garden.

The planting throughout the garden, which extends to 2.5 acres (1 hectare), is for all year round interest and includes many bulbs. In spring, snowdrops, *Scillas* and hellebores, lead on to *Crocus* and *Narcissi*, followed by a glorious tapestry of colourful tulips, which in turn make way for naturalised Snakeshead Fritillaries, *Camassias* and Martagon lilies.

In May, the garden is full of self-seeded *Aquilegias* of every colour imaginable, complemented by flowering sweet rocket *Hesperis matrionalis*.

There is also a topiary garden and alongside the banks of a cascading stream great swathes of the blue and white flowering Siberian Iris *Iris siberica*. Elsewhere, *Clematis*, *Amelanchier*, *Cercis*, *Prunus* and *Viburnum* bring flower and perfume to the air, only to be followed by over sixty-five different varieties of rose.

◀ Views to the paddocks beyond the garden

Stone House Garden in spring

❋ SUDELEY CASTLE GARDENS

Human occupation on this site dates back more than 1,000 years, and no wonder, given its superb setting within the Cotswolds and extensive views of the surrounding hills. Much of the infrastructure viewed by visitors today, including the castle and ruined tithe barn, dates from the fifteenth-century and provides a glorious backdrop to ten organically managed gardens which extend over an area of approximately fourteen acres.

Damaged during the Civil War, the castle was allowed to fall into dereliction, until, in the nineteenth century, it was purchased by the Dent family who began to sympathetically restore the property and create the gardens. One of the finest is the Queen's Garden, which contains an outstanding collection of old-fashioned English roses arranged around a central pool with balustrade, and bordered on two sides by magnificent close-clipped double yew hedges planted in 1860, which are in turn bordered by a series of topiary cones of gold and green foliage. ▸

The Elizabethan Knot Garden

Elegant ruins of the old tithe barn ▸

❀ SUDELEY CASTLE GARDENS

◀ Within and around the remains of the tithe barn, fragrant climbers clamber over the walls, whilst extensive borders, full of foliage and flower, surround its foundations, creating a romantic and peaceful atmosphere, reminiscent perhaps of the Victorian ruin the castle once was.

These two gardens alone would be enough to satisfy even the most enthusiastic garden visitor, but there is more to Sudeley . . . much more. A Victorian kitchen garden helps to preserve rare and traditional varieties of vegetables, a wildflower walk encourages butterflies and bees, and there are scented arbours and walkways galore. One of the latest features to be added to the landscape is an Elizabethan knot garden, designed by Jane Fearnley-Whittingstall in 1995; it takes its inspiration from the pattern decorating a dress worn by Queen Elizabeth I.

This is a garden of the past and of the future, with lots of 'ideas to steal' which could be adapted to fit many domestic-sized gardens. It will also inspire those on the lookout for unusual plants, be they white wisterias, oriental clematis, an ancient mulberry tree, or the delightful *Calycanthus occidentalis*, a Californian shrub with aromatic leaves and bright red summer flowers.

The Queen's Garden

❊ THE OLD RECTORY

Garden writer and designer Mary Keen has been gardening at The Old Rectory in Duntisbourne Rous since 1983. Over that time, she has created a two-acre horticultural delight, full of rare and unusual plants, all year round interest and – above all else – atmosphere. This is not a garden forced to stand to attention, with manicured lawns and weed-free borders, more a calming, peaceful palette of colours and textures, where plants are allowed to do their own thing. Of course, it helps if you know what 'their own thing' is, so you can plant them deliberately to do just that, and this is where Mary comes into her own, for her knowledge and understanding of plants is first class.

At the heart of the garden is the old schoolhouse and with its selection of gardening books and magazine articles, many written by Mary herself, it makes for a good launch pad for any tour of the garden. A well-planned garden should not give itself away lightly, you must never be allowed to see it all at once; each turn in a path, every archway through a hedge, should open up new vistas, new features, new moods, and the garden at The Old Rectory has been designed to do this to perfection. So from the relative calm of the front lawn one descends into the exuberance of the Summer Garden, passing an auricular theatre along the way. ▸

The Old Rectory

◀ Here, a St Andrew's Cross of paths, radiating off a central copper pot surrounded by fastigiate box pillars *Buxus* 'Greenpeace', provides four irregular-shaped beds which are filled with flowering shrubs underplanted with successional colour from tulips, honesty, paeonies, campanulas, salvias, penstemons and dahlias.

From here, there are several options to follow. Beyond the pool is a shrub dell with several members of the Rosaceae family – *Malus*, *Crataegus* and *Sorbus*, surrounded in early spring by snowdrops and anemones.

Or the path through the tool shed leads past hellebore beds to the latest feature created by Mary, a pictorial meadow on the site of the old herbaceous border. Pictorial meadows use differing annual wildflower mixes to create a tapestry of informal colour all summer long. Mary's mix includes cornflowers, poppies and larkspur and the effect is like brightly coloured confetti, particularly appropriate given the meadow is overlooked by the idyllic Cotswold-stone Saxon Church which stands close by.

◀ Successional planting in The Summer Garden   Pictorial meadow

❃ THROUGHAM COURT

On first arrival at Througham Court, all is as you might expect; a fine stone-built house dating from the seventeenth century and attractive views to the rolling Cotswold hills beyond the Holy Brook valley. In the foreground, glimpsed through the gate, is a garden bearing all the hallmarks of a traditional Arts and Crafts garden – flagstone terraces, sunken garden with borders, lawns and topiary – and indeed it is, laid out by Norman Jewson around 1930. Then, just as you begin to feel comfortable in your surroundings, you note the garden gate, a whirling, tumbling, pulsating design of roulette wheels, dice and stock exchange extremes, portraying the laws of probability and risk. It is the first of many thought-provoking and exciting garden features designed by Througham's twenty-first century owner Dr Christine Facer, a scientist, leading authority on malaria, landscape designer and someone who is inspired by scientific facts, genetics, numbers and patterns found in nature. 'I bought the property because of the historic Arts and Crafts garden, but then I realised there were spaces around the garden where I could experiment with contemporary design.' ▶

Bold colours contrast with the surrounding landscape

Garden of Cosmic Evolution ▶

◀ Today, Througham's intimate mix of conventional and contemporary garden design may at first seem unsettling, but then, as you tour the garden, it becomes stimulating as you search for meanings and explanations. References to Fibonacci abound and his sequential numbering system not only appears naturally within the petals of flowers but is found in the planting schemes created by Christine. Fibonacci's Walk uses white-barked birch *Betula Jacquemontii* to project the sequence. Elsewhere, Ancaster-stone spheres represent planets within the Garden of Cosmic Evolution and, in the Eclipse Shadow Bed, black grasses create dark shadows from which flowering *Cosmos* 'Astronaut' shines like stars in the night sky. Even in relatively conventional parts of the garden, the rules are constantly being broken with the use of asymmetry and unconventional colour combinations. Steps that access changing levels within the garden are covered in pillar-box-red artificial turf, Shona Watts banners flutter on the flanks of the surrounding hills and spirals of black bamboo create an inspirational maze. Charles Jencks had described Througham as 'A fascinating garden . . . the composition is absolutely brilliant', and indeed it is.

Unconventional but inspirational

❧ TORTWORTH COURT

Along with Westonbirt and Batsford Arboretum, Lord Ducie's tree collection at Tortworth Court, positioned on the western edge of the Cotswolds overlooking the Severn Vale near Wotton-under-Edge, was also established during the nineteenth century and in terms of diversity it was at one point believed to have been superior to both. Sadly, history has not treated it kindly, and from the 1930s until the 1990s, it went through long periods of neglect, during which many of the original Victorian plantings were lost. However, more recently, both court and arboretum have been restored by the Four Pillars Hotel Group and an inventory of the remaining plant collection has revealed a large number of both rare and champion trees (biggest of their kind in Britain) still in existence, including a magnificent Caucasian Elm *Zelkova carpinifolia*, the original Corkscrew hazel *Corylus avellana* 'Contorta', made famous as the twisted walking stick of the music-hall act, Sir Harry Lauder, and a fine specimen of paper-bark maple *Acer griseum*.

Areas of the original Ducie landscape, including a walk to the lake are still not fully open to the public, but even so there is much to enjoy here, particularly for those with a passion for trees. ▸

Tortworth Court

❁ TORTWORTH COURT

◀ Tortworth's most famous tree, however, lies not in the arboretum, but half a mile away, adjacent to the village church. For here is what I can only describe as probably one of the most venerable trees in Western Europe – the Tortworth Sweet Chestnut. Now, some ancient trees, despite their considerable age, neither have the stature or majesty to match their years, but the Tortworth Chestnut does not disappoint and has everything one would expect of a living organism which was a 'notable tree' in the time of King Stephen, around 1135, and some say may even have been planted by the Romans! Its great hulk, home to countless generations of bats and owls and bearing the scars of centuries-old battles with woodpeckers, insects, fungi and even fire, sprawls across the ground, its great limbs taking root where they repose. It is quite simply magnificent and what's more, it looks good for at least another 1,000 years!

◀ Paper-bark maple *Acer griseum* in the arboretum

The Tortworth Sweet Chestnut

❋ TRULL HOUSE GARDEN

The *Oxford English Dictionary* states that 'trull' actually means 'a lady of the night', a female of ill repute; it was a common enough word in sixteenth-century England. There is, however, another meaning, one which extends back to Saxon England and refers to an enclosure, or ring of trees, planted to denote the boundary of a farm or land holding. The ring at Trull House is of beech trees, some of them hundreds of years old and they encircle the 550 acres of farmland that surround the house and garden.

The present Trull House was constructed out of locally quarried Cotswold stone in 1841. To the side of the house, craggy and pock-marked stone ruins suggest an earlier dwelling of great antiquity. Do not be fooled, for this is a late-Victorian, early-Edwardian creation, a folly built of porous tufa stone and just one of several intriguing garden features to be found here. On the lawn directly in front of the house, is what at first glance appears to be the top of a submerged dovecot; it is, in fact, a beautiful, ornate Cotswold-tiled well cover. ▸

Trull House, with ornate well cover in foreground

Ivy-clad dovecote on the main lawn ▸

❀ TRULL HOUSE GARDEN

◄ This well is reputed to be the deepest in Gloucestershire and has never run dry.

Almost all the garden dates back to the early years of the twentieth century and includes a delightful sunken water-lily pool and a sunken rockery full of alpines and perennials. To the side and back of the house are two walled gardens, an outer and an inner one, with a series of sheltered 'corridor gardens' nestling between the walls. In summer, close-cut grass paths meander between serpentine borders overflowing with drifts of Oxford-and Cambridge-blue delphiniums, iris and campanulas, intermingled with pink and white paeonies, digitalis, alliums and poppies.

Here and there, little doorways in the walls tease with glimpses through to other garden rooms, each one quite different to its neighbour. A small orchard, an ancient iron pergola clothed in a colossal Rambling Rector rose and specimen trees and shrubs, including a superb specimen of a rare Chinese *Clerodendrum trichotomum*, all add to the enjoyment of this tranquil garden.

Serpentine borders wind between two garden walls

✿ UPTON HOUSE

I like gardens that are full of surprises and the National Trust property of Upton House holds one of the best garden surprises in the Cotswolds. The house is situated on a plateau and the gardens immediately surrounding it are, on first inspection, rather flat and uninteresting, with only one or two fine Lebanon cedars, which flank the main lawn to the rear of the house, worthy of comment.

However, do not be disheartened, for beyond the lawn what appears at first to be a ha-ha, separating lawn from pasture, suddenly drops away to reveal a whole valley of gardens completely hidden from view. The escarpment immediately below the lawn is south-facing and has been turned into a series of hot terraces known as the Mediterranean Banks and contains an excellent collection of plants from warmer regions of the world including the Californian tree poppy *Romneya coulteri* with its flamboyant 'poached-egg' flowers and great clumps of Oxford-blue Agapanthus from South Africa. ▶

Bed full of colour lead to the lake

❈ UPTON HOUSE

◀ The banks give way to a National Collection (NCCPG) of asters that boasts more than twenty species and 100 cultivars. Vegetable and fruit gardens lie below and then in the bottom of the valley there is a small lake bordered by lush foliage plants. To the eastern end of the valley, there are herbaceous borders packed with colour, and to the west, a series of small formal gardens, at least one of which is given over to roses.

Lord and Lady Bearsted laid out the ornamental gardens in the 1920s to a design created by Kitty Lloyd-Jones. 700 years before, monks from St Sepulchre's near Warwick had created at least five stewponds in the valley and grown fruit and vegetables. A grotto positioned towards the western end of the garden is still known today as 'Monk's Well' and from its mouth a natural spring flows through a delightful bog garden fringed with rheums, hostas, rodgersias, lysichiton and gunnera.

The strength of the gardens at Upton House lie in their diversity, both of plants and planting styles, which means this is a garden to return to and at differing times of year, be it spring, summer or autumn.

◀ The valley below the main lawn   Productive gardens slope down to the water's edge

❄ UPTON WOLD

When the present owners Ian and Caroline Bond came to Upton Wold in 1973, there was little garden to speak of, just two fine yews, some apple trees and a very beautiful view sweeping away to the east of the house down into a valley and then up a tree-clad Cotswold escarpment in the distance. From day one, the Bonds knew that whatever garden they created they had to ensure this fine view became an integral part of it. Thirty-six years on, and with the help of the late Brenda Colvin and Hal Moggridge along the way, they have achieved their objective handsomely. From the flag-stone terrace in front of the house, wide steps fringed with dwarf cotoneaster lead to a stepped lawn, bordered by close-clipped yew hedges which train the eye across a ha-ha to the all important vista beyond.

Step off the lawn, through openings in the yew to either side and you enter a succession of 'garden rooms', each with its own character and design. A formal canal garden, complete with fountain and weeping mulberry tree at each corner of the rectangular canal, leads through to the Hidden Garden, an area of light and shade where choice shrubs and trees, including many fine magnolias and a pocket-handkerchief tree *Davidia involucrata* – which eventually flowered after twenty years – are planted within a succession of glades. ▶

Herbaceous borders full of pastel shades

The Canal Garden ▶

◀ Walks of *Malus* 'John Downie' and stilted hornbeam, flanked by white, red and black herbaceous borders, bring both height and softness to the fruit and vegetable garden, which has at its heart an arbour draped with clematis and roses. Beyond, and through pillared gates topped with attractive metal scrolls of leaves, lies the Woodland Garden and one of the UK's National Collections (NCCPG) of *Juglans* (walnuts), which currently contains nearly 200 cultivars. Elsewhere, a pond and wild garden are approached from the end of long herbaceous borders full of pastel shades and silver-blue foliage. Adding further interest to this area is a fine sculpture by Emily Young and a delightful low trickling rill which designates the boundary between border and pathway.

Arbour draped with clematis and roses

❁ WESTONBIRT ARBORETUM

Without doubt one of the finest collections of trees in Britain is to be found at Westonbirt in the National Arboretum, located a few miles south of the attractive 'antiques town' of Tetbury. Over the last twenty years it has become one of the major visitor attractions of the Cotswolds and rightly so, for it really is a spectacular landscape.

The original trees of the arboretum (many of which survive to this day) were planted in 1829 by wealthy Gloucestershire landowner, Robert Holford. After his death, his son, Sir George Holford, and other family members continued to manage and expand the arboretum with trees collected from all over the temperate world. In 1956 the Forestry Commission became responsible for managing the collection on behalf of the nation and more than fifty years later that is still the case.

Today, the number of arboreal specimens exceeds 18,000, spread over an area of approximately 240 hectares (600 acres) and accessed by a series of 'easy on the legs' waymarked trails and footpaths. ▸

Acer Glade in autumn

◄ Along each trail interpretative panels identify some of the biggest, oldest and most interesting trees in the collection. The overall effect is both beautiful and fascinating and easily enjoyed by those just out for a walk in pleasant countryside as well as by those with a particular interest in woody plants.

Such is the scale of Westonbirt that it is not possible to see everything in just one visit. However, members of the Friends of Westonbirt Arboretum charity run a voluntary advisory service from a splendid, recently constructed, oak-framed hall and will suggest the best areas in which to walk on the day of your arrival.

Autumn is probably one of the most visually pleasing times to visit, when thousands of Japanese maples, Persian ironwoods and American hickories, put on magical displays of leaf colour. Spring too is particularly attractive when magnolias, rhododendrons and azaleas bloom on large tracts of naturally deposited acidic loam. Having said that, the sheer size and diversity of the collection means there is always colour and interest, whatever time of year you choose to visit.

◄ An October walk in Silkwood

Rhododendrons and azaleas near Savill Glade

✤ WESTONBIRT SCHOOL GARDEN

It will be, I am sure, no surprise to learn that both Westonbirt Arboretum and the grounds of Westonbirt House (School) have a common ancestry. They both owe their existence to one family – Holford – an ancient family with lineage back to the Normans.

It was Robert Stayner Holford who, in the 1830s, commenced work on the parkland and – as he called it – his 'Pleasure Grounds' surrounding Westonbirt House. There is some suggestion that, in the early stages, he was advised by landscape designer William Sawrey Gilpin. Certainly the parkland reflected the 'picturesque' style of the day, much used by Gilpin, and as such became a 'contrived natural' landscape, interspersed with carefully placed individual trees or groups of trees, which helped focus the eye to a series of vistas beyond.

By contrast, the Pleasure Grounds were highly cultivated, with lawns, ornamental plantings and architecture and included a walled 'Italian Garden' with sumptuous domed pavilions and walls, which contained flues and could be heated to protect tender plants in winter. ▸

Sumptuous domed pavilions   Westonbirt Church – part of the garden landscape ▸

✤ WESTONBIRT SCHOOL GARDEN

◀ This was the work of Henry Edward Hamlen, a pupil of Italian architect Lewis Vulliamy. Holford also commissioned Hamlen to design many of Westonbirt's rockeries, grottos, water features, statuary and hothouses – for orchid and amaryllis cultivation.

Although crumbling in places, most of these features, including one of the glasshouses, are still in existence today, as is Westonbirt church and the old village pond, which were absorbed into the garden landscape when Holford cleared the original Westonbirt village in the 1850s. It all makes for a fascinating garden visit which transcends many of the gardening fashions of the last 170 years. A grand formal terrace, bordered by ornate balustrades and herbaceous beds, runs in an east-west direction and is bisected by an avenue and several flights of steps, which lead away from the house and towards a circular lily pool overlooked by a canopied stone seat. The views from here back to the house are impressive and somehow reminiscent of the château-style found in the Loire Valley.

From this point there are gems in every direction; pools and statuary in the Mercury Garden, the stylish architecture of the Italian Garden and a beautiful Victorian wrought-iron pergola overrun with jasmine, which leads from the Italian Garden back towards the main south lawn where fine specimen trees, including a magnificent maidenhair tree *Ginkgo biloba*, stand proud.

Long vista to the house